Brian Rust's
Guide to
Discography

Brian Rust's Guide to Discography

BRIAN RUST

Discographies, Number 4   GREENWOOD PRESS

WESTPORT, CONNECTICUT • LONDON, ENGLAND

Library of Congress Cataloging in Publication Data

Rust, Brian A   L
    Brian Rust's guide to discography.

    (Discographies ; no.4 ISSN 0192-334X)
    Bibliography: p.
    Includes index.
        1.   Music—Discography—Theory, methods, etc.
2.   Music—Discography—Bibliography.   3.   Cataloging
of sound recordings.   I.   Title.   II.   Series.
ML111.5.R87   016.7899'12   79-6827
ISBN 0-313-22086-7 (lib. bdg.)

Library of Congress Catalog Card Number: 79-6827

ISBN: 0-313-22086-7
ISSN: 0192-334X

First published in 1980

Greenwood Press
A division of Congressional Information Service, Inc.
88 Post Road West, Westport, Connecticut 06881

Printed in the United States of America

10 9 8 7 6 5 4 3 2 1

CONTENTS

ILLUSTRATIONS

Sample pages from significant discographies

PREFACE

IT IS now something like half a century since the word "discography" was introduced, and in that time a considerable number of works in the category of discographies have been published in one form or another. Some are little more than résumés of the record companies' catalogs; others show the often incredible dedication of their compilers to their chosen subject. This book sets out to define the purposes and functions of a discography and to show what is involved in the compilation of one. Also included is a history of the science—for that is what it is—a bibliography of the major discographies, a reference guide to the major and most significant record companies and their various products, and a glossary of the terms in common usage in discography.

For as long as I can remember, I have been fascinated by the process of listing details of records. As a child, I would make catalogs of records I had, or wished I had, complete with as much information as the labels and the discs themselves provided. At times I would amuse myself, in a kind of never-never land, by making lists of records that I wished some company would produce. From time to time, by sheer coincidence, these wishes were granted, or I would discover, as I acquired more extensive knowledge, that the desired records had existed all along. I would like to think that the broadening and deepening of that fascination of long ago qualify me, as a discographer, to present this book.

Acknowledgments are normally due to others in a work of this kind, and in this case I feel that my thanks should go to those other discographers whose works are listed and discussed in chapter 7. Most of them provided the inspiration for, and many the substance of my own discographies.

To those who offered useful help and constructive criticism, though not themselves discographers in the active sense, I must express my sincere gratitude: Paul C. Burgess; the late I.V. de Yorke; John Wadley; Renate Warburg; the late Michael Wyler; and particularly my wife, Mary, for compiling the index and for her understanding and patience.

Brian Rust's
Guide to
Discography

1

Purpose and Function of Discography

ALTHOUGH THE word discography has been in use since at least the fourth decade of the twentieth century, it does not seem to merit inclusion in the majority of dictionaries and other works of reference published in the English language. It may be regarded as a somewhat ugly word, but in view of its meaning of "writing about discs" (from the Greek *diskos*, a disc, and *graphein*, to write), it would be difficult to devise a neater one for the purpose.

From this term, of course, derives the adjunct of discographer, one concerned with writing about discs, the discs themselves being any medium for the preservation of sound. As with many words which begin their life by referring to a specific object, "discography" and related terms now loosely cover recordings on cylinders and even tape.

Writing about records in the discographical sense does not, of course, involve discussion of the merits and demerits of the actual sound recorded; discographers are not, or at least should not be, critics. That is beyond their function. A discography is simply a work of reference to all the known recordings by a given performer or group of performers or by those coming within certain limits of style, category, period, or composition.

There are those to whom a phonograph or gramophone record is no more than a means of providing entertainment at will and in accordance with the choice and mood of the individual. Such people seem to find difficulty in understanding the need, and thus the purpose, of discography; that is, the science of research into what has been recorded for posterity, by whom, when, where, and on what makes of record, with precise details of the various numerical identifications allocated by the companies concerned. These skeptics, even cynics, find no similar problems understanding listings and detailed accounts of the appearance, dimensions, age, and whereabouts of accepted works of art in painting and sculpture, for example, which reflect the culture of the· civilizations that produced and fostered them. Nor does the existence of large books devoted to the documentation and current market value of postage stamps, objects of questionable artistic value, trouble them. Yet these good people become quite confused and bewildered at the sight of a discography, especially if— as is usually the case—it is primarily concerned with what are tiresomely often dismissed as "scratchy old 78s." For who on earth wants to know about such things, which can only accommodate about three or four minutes of playing time on each side (and then require changing), and which are at once so bulky and heavy, yet so fragile?

The answer is, of course, the students of some particular aspect of art or drama, or of history in the twentieth century; aspiring musicians, seeking knowledge from the audible, authentic works of the great masters of their art, living and dead; the playwrights, theater, film, and television producers, looking for music that will accurately set the scene in some forthcoming production; and, of course, that most strange individual, the avid collector of some or all of these kinds of music. To all these, discography is by no means something to be sneered at as "analytical bookkeeping" and dismissed as mere musical philately, as some I have heard do. It is the detailed documentation of the history—of art, politics, world events—of the twentieth century itself.

We cannot say how Julius Caesar sounded when addressing the Roman senate, or Jesus Christ on the Mount, or Abraham Lincoln at Gettysburg. We have only the impressions of those present who wrote of what they heard when Jenny Lind sang, or Frédéric Chopin played in the Salle Pleyel. We can, however, when so inclined, determine exactly what the style of oratory of Winston Churchill, Franklin Delano Roosevelt, Adolf Hitler, or Benito Mussolini was. We can delight in the majesty of Enrico Caruso or the limpid beauty of Nellie Melba, or thrill to the power of the New York Philharmonic Orchestra under the baton of Arturo Toscanini or to the sonorous trumpet of Louis Armstrong, according to our wish. We can recall the happiness of our youth with a record of a favorite dance tune, or evoke the memory of a loved one with some favorite song. We can, that is, if we know where to look for them.

The obvious place to look is the current catalogs of the record companies or the summaries published by Schwann in New York and *Gramophone* magazine in London. These will tell us what is currently available. If what we are looking for is no longer in circulation, however, we need a more comprehensive reference book, one which will offer alternatives and more information, such as the date on which our required record was made (an important point for the meticulous producer anxious to avoid the pitfalls of anachronism) and full details of all the forms in which any title or group of titles were issued.

A discography is often useful to the theater, film, or television producer and scriptwriter of a "period" play in which incidental music must be of the right era. It is quite extraordinary how often the music of a production of this kind is completely out of character with the point in history of the action. Thus, we see couples dancing in a Chicago speakeasy in the Prohibition era to music that had not been written, played in a style that recalls the late 1930s or even later. In the film of Sir Noël Coward's *Blithe Spirit*, made in England in 1946, there is a scene where a record of Irving Berlin's waltz *Always* is played. We see the record being taken from its cover, although the design of the label is of the style of a much earlier issue than even the earliest version could possibly be, and we hear a few bars played by a band instantly recognizable as being of ten or twenty years later. Similarly, in *The Great Caruso*, Mario Lanza in the title role is seen playing what purports to be Caruso's own record of the ballad *Because*—on a twelve-inch record, with a label for which Caruso did not record, and in English. (The real Caruso made *Because* on a ten-inch disc, in French.) It may be considered overfastidious to dwell on points such as these, but they are nevertheless just as absurd as if a film set in World War I were to show the Red Baron flying a Messerschmit or the soundtrack of the same film showing the hero on his last night of furlough intoning *I'll Be Seeing You*. More recently, a number of British television producers have asked me for help on questions relating to the right kind of period-setting music, and by referring them to extant discographies, I was able to set them on the right track, literally. Thus, the incidental contemporary music heard at times through the popular series "Upstairs, Downstairs" was always absolutely correct, and caused no anachronistic discords, but served its purpose of lending authenticity and natural color to the action at that time. In short, we need a discography.

It will perhaps be argued at this point that the contents of a discography, unless it be one of some artist currently before the public, are by their nature no longer obtainable. This is true, if by "obtainable" is meant "from a store dealing in new records." But there exist throughout the world libraries of all kinds of records to which the public has access, and there are thousands of enthusiastic collectors who, among them, can account for almost any record any casual individual is likely to need, and who, without infringing on copyright laws if the records required are over fifty years old, are usually quite willing to copy them on tape or cassette. Such collectors can usually be contacted through the multitude of specialist magazines (see Appendix II) or the shops dealing in the unusual, the rare, or at least the not generally obtainable (see Appendix I).

If one is a keen admirer of some particular type of music or other recorded sound, of course, a detailed professionally produced discography is a *sine qua non*. The admirer of the art of singing, let us say, whether he or she is a singer or not, will be attracted to the voices of the great singers not only of the present, of whom there are adequate recordings readily available from any good music store, but of the past as well. Our singing enthusiast will perhaps have heard a record of Enrico Caruso, John McCormack, Fedor Chaliapin, Tito Schipa, Geraldine Farrar, Alma Gluck, or some little-known artist whose voice is nevertheless sheer magic. How can he find out exactly what else has been recorded by these singers, and, as a point of historical interest, when they recorded them, where, and on what issues? In the case of collectors and enthusiasts of jazz and dance music, it is a positive aid to intelligent appreciation, despite allegations to the contrary frequently voiced by those lacking both intelligence and appreciation, to know exactly who is playing that well-constructed, perhaps entirely improvised, variation on the theme, who wrote the arrangement that so accurately matches the intentions of the composer, who is the vocalist so tenderly projecting the lyrics of this romantic ballad but to whom the label gives no credit.

If such details are anathema to those to whom jazz and dance music are themselves anathema, it might be worth gently remarking that these musical forms are gaining wider acceptance every year throughout the world, that they are acknowledged generally as representing America's major contribution to twentieth-century musical culture, and that they deserve such close attention. In exactly the same way as discographers attempt to pin down the exact identities of each member of jazz and dance bands of the past, Mozart enthusiasts examine the very manuscript paper on which the master wrote his incomparable scores, even locating the source of the paper, the watermarks, and the dates between which he could have purchased it. The ordering and dating of his work, even approximately, was first undertaken by a Viennese mineralogist with the meticulous approach befitting his occupation. This musical biographer was inspired by an intense admiration for the music of Mozart, who had died nine years before he was born. He was Ludwig von Köchel (1800-1877), and were he living today, no doubt he would have made an excellent discographer, perhaps of recordings of Mozart's music.

When the recording of sound passed from the realms of fantasy into the bounds of possibility and certainty, during the latter half of the nineteenth century, the scientists chiefly responsible were the American-born Thomas Alva Edison, and the German immigrant Emile Berliner, who settled in Washington in the 1880s and conducted his experiments there. Each approached the problem of recording and reproducing sound in very different ways, each with a different objective: Edison favored a system whereby the recording stylus *indented* the sound pattern into a tinfoil-covered *cylinder*, later changing to a wax one, whereas Berliner devised a method of *cutting* a track in 'a zinc *disc* covered with a fatty substance, then immersing it in an acid bath to fix the sound pattern permanently on the disc, through contact of the acid with the zinc exposed by the recording stylus. From this several hundred copies could be produced through a further process of making a negative copy by electrolysis. Edison would have to engage his artists and performers to record the same selection many times over, but initially, his objective was not to produce something of entertainment or artistic value so much as to replace a human secretary as an aid to commerce. Berliner's intent was to produce a means of home entertainment, and little else. He seldom recorded historically interesting personalities of the day delivering speeches, whereas Edison sent an emissary to London in the late 1880s to enshrine their voices forever. Neither of these inventors could have foreseen that within half a century or less of their deaths, their products would have achieved the status of valuable historical documents, comparable in their way with original printings by William Caxton, first folios of Shakespeare, and early photographs of mid-nineteenth century celebrities by Louis Daguerre. Still less could they have dreamed that their work would merit the close examination accorded them by the twentieth-century phenomenon, the discographer.

When compiling a discography, some detailed knowledge of the background history of the industry is essential. One of the most important books on this is *The Fabulous Phonograph*, by Roland Gelatt (New York: Cassell, 1956). Another is Jerrold Moore's *A Voice in Time*, a biography of Fred Gaisberg, the American impresario and recording engineer who was Berliner's emissary to Europe (based in London) from the summer of 1898 on. This was published in London by Hamish Hamilton in 1976. A third major work is *From Tin Foil to Stereo*, by Oliver Read and Walter L. Welch (Indianapolis: Howard W. Sams & Co., Inc., 1959). This delves further into the more technical side of the story of sound recording, and gives much coverage to radio, sound pictures, juke boxes, and so on, with illustrations of all kinds of *machines*, none at all of the artists, and much purely scientific detail of no discographical interest at all. Equally important is a knowledge of the appearance of the various types of records issued by the multitude of companies and their overseas associates and subsidiaries, their labels, type-faces, numbering systems, and such details as the various kinds of "run-off" grooves that differ from company to company and from age to age. All of these factors are invaluable in determining the date of recording, however approximately. The task of a jazz discographer, or that of a dance music discographer, is more complex than, let us say, that of an operatic or other more serious music historian, because the latter are not concerned with such minutiae as the personnel of accompanying orchestras, nor do they often find themselves confronted with puzzling pseudonyms. It is commonplace in the world of popular records to find some well-known band or soloists masquerading under a pseudonym on a rival label to the one with which they hold binding contracts. Some labels use the same pseudonym to cover every band appearing in their catalogs, while others apply a variety of pseudonyms to the same artist or band. Some subsidiaries of American parent companies in England and in some Continental European countries suppress the matrix number—the serial applied to each recording at the time of, or sometimes in advance of, the session—and substitute a number of their own. Others merely add their own identification number to one already *in situ,* which has been known to add to the confusions and perplexities of research in the past.

Despite the absence of pitfalls such as these where operatic and other vocalists' discographies are concerned, the rarity of the records themselves naturally provides problems no less difficult, sometimes even impossible, to solve. This is simply because documentary evidence of the sessions in many cases no longer exists. The files of the old Victor Talking Machine Company, and its successor, the RCA (Radio Corporation of America) Victor Records Division, are commendably complete, but those of other companies of the earliest years of the recording industry have mostly disappeared into the mists of time.

As many of these lost documents must have borne witness to the erstwhile existence of recordings of interest and cultural importance, their reconstruction as far as possible from close examination of published examples becomes a matter of important historical research. The publication of complete accounts of what was recorded, by whom, where, and when on various labels in America since the end of World War II is already being undertaken by various presses; and as will be seen in chapter 7, there have been several other label-listings that for their completeness, accuracy, and comprehensiveness must rank with the discographies of artists and various kinds of music included under the same heading.

Perhaps the most widespread function of a discography of an artist, group of artists, or style of music is to aid an appreciation of the development of their art. As we have seen, personnels of bands and accompanying units are the special concern of jazz and dance music enthusiasts and collectors, and the entry of numbers allocated by the companies for their own convenience and that of their selling agents and ultimately their customers becomes a necessary, but not vitally important, adjunct to the appreciation of that art. Many a discographer, whether experienced or novice, must have had to suffer the slings and arrows of critics who believe that a discographer is principally, if not solely, concerned with purely numerical details of a record and that its musical merit or lack of it is not his concern. I have myself been the recipient of these verbal missiles, but have been at some pains to explain by the spoken and the written word that knowledge of the numerical details of a given record is desirable to place it in the context of other similar recordings. It is not a direct aid to artistic appreciation, but a bridge across the stream of knowledge leading to that appreciation.

The most important factor in any discography is the dating of each entry. Once we have the various numbers on a record before us, with a little experience it becomes possible to put at least an approximate date on it. On listening to the records, we can then determine how the style or character of the performance relates to that by the same artist on other later or earlier recordings, or, if it is that artist's only recording, we can assess his or her qualities compared with contemporary recordings by other artists working in the same medium. For example, it is very interesting to compare the methods characteristic of tenor Enrico Caruso at the outset of his operatic career in 1902 and at the end of his life, when he made his last recordings in 1920. Not only have the recording techniques improved, although on both occasions the acoustic method of singing or playing into a metal funnel was used, but the voice and its flexibility, projection, and intonation have changed almost beyond recognition. Both are obviously the voice of a great singer, but no one, even a complete tyro, could mistake the one for the other. A similar degree of change can be discerned in the case of the most popular singer the world has ever known, and over a much shorter period of time: Bing Crosby, at the outset of his career with Paul Whiteman's orchestra, making his first solo record (anonymously) in 1927, has a lighter, much less sonorous voice than when recording three years later with Gus Arnheim and his orchestra. The vibrant depth of tone that caught the attention, not to say the hearts, of countless admirers of both sexes in the following four decades was then beginning to show. Knowing the dates of these recordings enables us to compare, balance, and assess, for better or for worse, the facets of art, be it classical or popular. The same applies, of course, to the work of jazz musicians whose recording and, as a rule, public life extended over a number of years. Comparison of the methods of Duke Ellington at the outset of his career as a bandleader, arranger, and composer in 1924 with those of three, ten, twenty, or any other number of years later is positively startling.

Another use of discographical material in a purely scientific field is to compare and judge the recording techniques themselves. A Victor or Columbia record, for example, made in the first decade of the century will not only bear little similarity to a record produced by the same or other companies a decade or so later, but even to each other. The ear

becomes attuned in time, of course, to the rather more brilliant Victor
sound of the 1900s compared to the somewhat thicker, solid tone of a
Columbia, and when Edison Diamond Discs—those quarter-inch thick
monsters, weighing two or three times as much as a standard record—
were introduced in 1912, they too bore their unmistakable auditory
characteristics (a precise clarity of the top frequencies and little or no
bass part at all). When the patents covering sound recording expired in
1916, many other companies were formed to expand the marriage of art
and science, and so we find the 1920s burgeoning with the beautifully
accurate, well-balanced Vocalion Red Record, the velvety new Columbia,
the shrill Pathé Actuelle, the incomparably rich, smooth, natural sounding
Victor and OKeh (the latter produced under the genius of Charles Hibbard),
and the distant, almost timorously thin sound of the Gennett product
of the Starr Piano Company in Richmond, Indiana. (Most of the other
companies had their head offices and/or their studios in New York.)

Then in 1924 came a very small label called Autograph, produced
in Chicago by Orlando R. Marsh, and the first electric recordings to be
put on sale. Marsh's previous recordings under the acoustic system were
quite acceptable, but the change to a primitive electric method produced
some of the most painfully distorted recordings in the entire history of
the industry. This is a great pity, as they were often of immense importance
in the story of recorded jazz, and included interesting work at the console
of the huge Wurlitzer organ in the Tivoli Cinema, Chicago, by the pioneer
Jesse Crawford, still regarded today in the organ music collecting world
as the greatest of them all. His Autograph records are adequate, no more,
but his later Victors, made electrically between 1925 and 1933, demonstrate
the vast progress in recording techniques during that decade.

Not all the companies extant early in 1925 could record by the revolutionary new method, of course. It was the property of the Western Electric
Company and was licensed to Victor and Columbia. It was a matter of
some two years before the smaller makes were able to develop their own
systems of recording with a microphone. Knowledge of and reference
to the numbering on these recordings shows which were made by which
system. Even as late as the spring of 1929, Columbia's inexpensive Harmony
subsidiary, and its sister labels Diva and Velvet Tone, were being made
by a strangely primitive-sounding acoustic system that made every record
sound as if it had been made in a matchbox by midgets. How and why
this was achieved is not known even to this day. The absence of the letter
W in a circle, stamped in the wax of electric Columbias and their subsidiary OKeh, gives the clue to the Harmony recording, even on records
pressed from Harmony masters in other countries with other trademarks.

In England and Continental Europe recording techniques were in exact
step with the United States, at least where the European branches were

concerned. Thus, German Odeon records, and others produced by arrangement with OKeh on such labels as Lindström, Beka, and Parlophon, were superb examples of the recording engineer's art. (German Brunswick records were tonally no better or worse than their American counterpart, but their manufacture was a sheer triumph—they had the appearance of a mirror or plate glass, and a smooth, velvety surface that produced no irritating hiss or rumble.) German pressings from the Deutsche Grammophon Aktiengesellschaft are also superb, and they have the added advantage of beautifully natural recording.

The British recording system that caused the greatest impact was that developed in 1931 by an Anglo-German named A.D. Blumlein. He is even said to have been working on stereophonic recording early in the thirties; but be that as it may, records made by his system have a fresh, natural sound in all registers that compares most favorably with anything made in later years. It is said that, quite apart from the unmatched excellence of the actual music, the excellence of these recordings, applied to the dance records by Ray Noble, the staff conductor at the EMI (Electric and Musical Industries) studios, were to some extent responsible for his being invited to New York in 1934 to direct a dance band there for public dancing, radio, and recording. Blumlein's system was denoted by a swastika, ironically enough, stamped in the wax on each side recorded by it, but soon after introduction a square was substituted. At first the Blumlein records were all "His Master's Voice," but the closing of the Columbia and Parlophone studios in various parts of London and centralizing them in a large Victorian house in the suburb of St. John's Wood meant that all subsequent recordings issued on these labels from masters made in Britain were in fact made by the same system.

During the 1930s, the recording industry in the United States was in the doldrums for much of the time. It had suffered grievous blows during the financial panic following the Wall Street disasters of the autumn of 1929, and the increasing popularity of radio added to its parlous position. The situation in Europe was similar, but less disastrous. At all events, by the mid-1930s, the major record companies in the United States were RCA Victor, the American Record Corporation (which accounted for Brunswick, Vocalion, and the inexpensive labels that had competed with each other in the booming 1920s in chain stores and others) and the newcomer, Decca. In Britain, at the outset of the decade, EMI, Decca, Crystalate, and Vocalion, with Edison Bell, Sterno, and Piccadilly trying to compete, accounted for most of the trade in records. There was also a British branch of Brunswick, but Decca absorbed this after Crystalate absorbed Vocalion. Then in 1937 EMI and Decca bought Sterno between them. By that time, Decca was already controlling Edison Bell, but only as a trade name, and Piccadilly also. Both of these makes had vanished as actual records.

In March 1937, Decca assumed control of Crystalate itself, so that at the outbreak of war in 1939, and for the duration, EMI and Decca were supreme. Except that by that time CBS had taken over the American Record Corporation with all its assets, including the various labels, and reactivated the dormant Columbia label, the position was similar in America: RCA, CBS, and Decca were the major companies.

The industry was climbing back to popularity when the American Federation of Musicians called on all its members to withhold their services from commercial recording unless the companies paid the AFM a royalty for the relief of unemployed musicians (it was held that the widespread use of records on radio and elsewhere was directly responsible for these unemployed). The companies refused, and for a little over a year in the case of Decca, two and one quarter years for RCA and CBS, no musical records could be produced. Vocal records with supporting choral groups were possible because these were not made by members of the Federation.

After the capitulation, conditions returned to normal, until a similar situation arose in 1947, and no instrumental records could be made until a new agreement was reached (more rapidly than previously). Therefore, for the first eight months of 1948, American popular singers and their choral colleagues dominated the new releases. Before the resumption of normal recording, however, CBS had introduced their revolutionary long-playing record, with minute grooves, playing speed of 33⅓ revolutions per minute, pressed in virtually unbreakable vinylite plastic. RCA, Decca, and the relative newcomer, Capitol, followed suit, producing also a seven-inch disc playing at 45 rpm principally for popular music. Recording since the end of the war in 1945 was more and more a matter of tape instead of wax or other kinds of disc. Distinguishing numbers that could help identify and determine the date of recording began to fall into disuse, at least where long-playing records were concerned. RCA Victor had tried to interest the public in just such a project in 1931, but their slow-speed standard-groove productions pressed in a rather gritty substance known as Victrolac, requiring special and necessarily expensive equipment to play, were of little appeal to the average buyer who could barely afford a normal 78 rpm disc at that time.

The introduction of the long-playing microgroove disc meant the obvious end of the shellac 78 rpm record. By the onset of the 1960s, it had become as obsolete as Edison's cylinders, which had continued in production until 1929 (Columbia, the other major cylinder make in the United States, had abandoned cylinders in the summer of 1912). The task of the discographer became more complex, as ornate albums containing the work of one or more artists over a period of years became commonplace—yet without numerical means of identification, how could their place in a discography be accurately assessed? In the case of re-issues from 78s, for historical or purely nostalgic purposes, these details are usually shown on the covers (known as "liners" in America and "sleeves" in England). However, in the majority of such cases, they are extracted from existing discographies, a further example of the function of a discographical work.

Compiling a discography of a modern artist's recordings, as I have said, is a task involving complications almost entirely unknown to the research worker concerned primarily with 78 rpm discs. One of the phenomena of present-day recording is the practice of splicing two or more sections of recorded tape together, making a unified performance from selected extracts from several. These may have been recorded at the same session, or they may not. The casual listener, if the splicing has been done expertly, seldom if ever notices the change, but it should be immediately obvious that an entry in a discography regarding recordings of this kind—a sort of musical jigsaw puzzle—becomes very difficult. Indeed, there was one case of an eminent operatic soprano who reached for a high note at the end of a record she was making, but for some reason she failed, and the recording was doomed for rejection. A little-known but very capable soprano was called in, however, to sing that one note as Madame X should have sung it, and the tiny scrap of tape on which it was recorded was skillfully inserted in the approximate place after the failed one had been removed. The record went on sale with full credit to Madame X and none whatever to her able substitute. This is perhaps a rather extreme example of the problems confronting a discographer of modern recordings, but it shows the kind of legerdemain that goes into producing a sophisticated work.

It is perhaps only fair to remark that in the 78 era, there was at least one comparable occasion when a famous British music-hall comedian was engaged to appear on an "all-star" record involving a number of his colleagues, supposedly at a party where they were called on in turn to sing or play something to amuse the "guests," in this case the members of the accompanying orchestra. The comedian was unable to appear at the last minute, but his lines in the script were spoken by one of the others with such incredible verisimilitude that when the absentee heard the published record, he is said to have been heard to mutter, "Marvellous what they can do nowadays—I wasn't even there."

In the case of modern "plastic surgery," of course, what the ear does not hear, or the eye does not see, the heart of a discographer and his readers will not grieve. Nevertheless, multitrack recordings openly known to be such can cause untidiness in presenting a discography, if nothing more. There are examples of a popular singer recording unaccompanied in Los Angeles, and a backing orchestra providing the accompaniment some days later in New York. This is an extension of the commonplace "gimmick" in the 1930s of inducing singers with sufficiently wide vocal range to make records of duets with themselves, the men singing both the tenor and the baritone parts. At least these were usually the result of one session. Artistically this gimmick has as much merit as a clever party trick, but its limit in those days was surely reached when an erstwhile boy soprano who had made successful records as such was recalled to the studios about a decade later, as a young man with a fully developed baritone voice, to sing duets with himself when younger.

In more recent times, of course, it has become quite usual for parts of a performance to be recorded on twenty-four-track tape, each track being the product of a different session on a different date from its fellows. Such sessions are sometimes spread over a period of weeks, even months. Thus a "pop" star could have committed his vocal art to a track on a tape in one month, the brass accompaniment added a week later, the strings prerecorded by several weeks, and the percussion any number of months later still. Similarly, with a symphony orchestra, the various sections could have been recorded on different dates, and the whole composite effect put on a stereo master for issue—which creates almost insuperable problems for the would-be discographer, whether of The Who or of the London Symphony Orchestra conducted by André Previn.

2

A Short History of the Science of Discography

THE WORD *discography* was used for the first time, as far as I can trace, in the title of a book devoted to "hot" jazz records. This was *Hot Discography*, by Charles Delaunay, published in Paris in 1936 by the Hot Club of France. It was not, of course, the first work published that listed all the then traceable records of a certain kind, but it does seem to lay fair claim to being the first to use the word as a description of its contents.

The first attempts at discographical listings of any kind seem to be those related to early operatic and vocal records, generally. These are almost certainly the first to appeal as collectors' items, and where there are keen collectors, there will be found, sooner or later, a comparable keenness for knowledge of the unknown, the unobtained, and eventually the unobtainable, human nature being what it is. The first public recognition of the existence of the record *collector*, in Great Britain at least, seems to have come with the June 1928 issue of *The Gramophone*, when the long-established feature, *Notes and Queries* under the editorship of "Piccolo" (H.F.V. Little, the Italian word for whose surname provided a pseudonym), was incorporated into a new feature known as *Collectors' Corner*. Originally, the feature's purpose was to help record purchasers obtain records that were not shown in the then current catalogs, or to advise them on the care of their machines. Under the new title, the emphasis was more and more on the collecting of old records, particularly those by great singers of the opening years of the century, with occasional reference to the artists of the music halls and musical theater productions of roughly the same period.

This was a fairly regular feature of *The Gramophone* until November 1930, after which it did not appear again until May 1931, and then over the signature of P. G. Hurst, who presided over it until March 1937. After a hiatus of four months, *Collectors' Corner* reappeared in August, a contribution from Leo Reimens of Holland. From that point on, various established collectors, always of vocal records by opera and concert singers, contributed occasional articles. It is interesting to note that one of the first cohesive attempts at a discography of any kind was undoubtedly the first rather rough listing of early operatic and vocal records generally by the Italian collector Roberto Bauer, in 1937. Yet it was always referred to then, and for a number of years afterwards, as a "listing."

The Gramophone can probably claim credit for publishing the first attempts at listing the records of a given artist in as much detail as was then considered essential. The April 1930 issue carried such an account of the known recordings of the Czech soprano Emmy Destinn, who had died the previous January. The author of the accompanying article, W. S. Meadmore, acknowledged with gratitude the help of, among others, H. F. V. Little. The contribution was the twenty-fifth in an intermittent series called *Gramophone Celebrities*, the preceding chapters being largely biographical, with some notes on the selected, and then readily available, records by the subject of the article.

The same periodical, in its issues for December 1931 and January 1932, carried an appreciation of the art of Nellie Melba, together with a listing—it was still known thus—of her records, in rather more detail than had been accorded to Emmy Destinn. The author was a thirty-two-year-old American, Henry McK. Rothermel, whose tragic death in a car accident coincided with the publication of the first installment of this appreciation of the singer he had admired so deeply, who had herself died the previous February. Other occasional "listings" of records by vocal celebrities of what became known as "the Golden Age of Singing" were published in *The Gramophone* in the years that followed, and in 1946 P. G. Hurst himself published a book entitled *The Golden Age Recorded*. It contained an anthology of the work on record of a number of outstanding singers, but it was never described as a discography.

The year 1936 not only witnessed the publication of Charles Delaunay's *Hot Discography*, referred to earlier. The so-called "Bible" of the dance-band profession in England, a weekly magazine called *The Melody Maker*, produced that year a book by Hilton R. Schleman called *Rhythm on Record* (London, 1936), which covered in nearly three hundred double-column pages biographical and roughly discographical notes on a wide selection of American, British, and some European dance music and jazz personalities, with many excellent glossy illustrations throughout.

Two years after his first attempt, Charles Delaunay produced a new version of *Hot Discography* (1938) and planned a third, but the outbreak of World War II delayed this. The remarkable fact is that neither this catastrophe nor the subsequent occupation of France by the Nazis, who were by training opposed to anything as "non-Aryan" as jazz, were able to suppress the eventual appearance of the third *Hot Discography* (1943), and after the war, Delaunay visited New York and sold the project of a *New Hot Discography* to Criterion Books, which appeared in 1948. In 1951 an attempt was made to present the definitive discography of jazz in all its forms in serial form, but this was never completed. Delaunay retired from the discographical scene. A special tribute must be paid to him for his tireless efforts at establishing who played what instrument or instruments on which records, especially when it is borne in mind that he was also working under the handicap of a foreign language.

Almost coincidental with the appearance of *New Hot Discography* came a revised and extended edition of *Historical Records*, by Roberto Bauer. This was published in London in 1947 by Sidgwick & Jackson. Its author died some twenty years later, but it remains at this writing the standard reference book for the recordings of singers of more than local fame who committed their art to records, at least up to the arbitrary "cut-off" date of 1908-1909.

It should not be assumed from the foregoing that vocal and jazz records are the only ones to have received detailed, or even cursory, discographical attention. The appearance in 1931 of the *Gramophone Shop Book,* listing a wide selection of records then available or only recently deleted, was a landmark in the presentation of a discography of serious orchestral and instrumental works, chiefly on American issues since it was pro- duced by the New York store whose name it bore. The encyclopedic work that covers serious works on record more fully, because current availability was looked on by the compilers as of no consequence, is the *World Encyclopaedia of Recorded Music*, by Francis F. Clough and G. J. Cuming, originally published in London in 1952 by Sidgwick & Jackson in association with the Decca Record Co. Ltd., and in New York by the London Gramophone Corporation. Several editions have been published since that date.

It is, nevertheless, true that jazz, and to a lesser extent, dance music generally, has commanded the attention of discographers more than any other form of music. There have, however, already been two editions of *Blues and Gospel Records, 1902-1942*, by W. J. Godrich and Robert M. W. Dixon, published privately in 1963 and by Storyville Publications some ten years later, and at this writing, a third edition is in preparation. A continuation of this work, covering the years from 1942 to the sixties, has been published semiprivately by Blues Unlimited; it was the work of the late Mike Ledbitter.

Charles Delaunay and Hilton Schleman laid the foundations of major discographical works on jazz and dance music, as we have seen; but between Delaunay's undercover edition of his *Hot Discography* in France during the occupation in 1943 and his American edition five years later, the one-time mayor of New Orleans, Orin Blackstone, produced a set of four books called *Index to Jazz*. These were published by the now-defunct jazz collectors' magazine *The Record Changer* in Fairfax, Virginia, from 1944 to 1948. Almost contiguously with this work, in England between July 1949 and January 1955, appeared six slim volumes of *Jazz Directory*, compiled by a team consisting of Albert McCarthy and David Carey, with Ralph G. V. Venables included on the first volume. The letters A through most of L were covered, and it was, of course, intended to complete the work to Z, but for various reasons this never took place. The first four volumes were published by the Delphic Press in the Hampshire village of Fordingbridge, but the last two bore the imprint of Cassell's of London.

During the 1950s, both Delaunay and Blackstone attempted to produce updated editions of their existing works, but neither succeeded in completing them. Without wishing to seem boastful, I might mention what is after all a matter of history, that I produced a series of books called *Jazz Records, 1897-1942*, over the years 1961 through 1978, the first two being privately published, the third by Storyville in Chigwell, Essex, England, in 1971, and the fourth by Arlington House, New York, in 1978. I have since authored similar volumes devoted to American dance bands, entertainment personalities (New York: Arlington House), and speeches by politicians, statesmen, sportsmen, and other public figures (Westport, Conn.: Greenwood Press) in the United States, and British dance bands, 1912 to 1939 (Chigwell, Essex, England: Storyville, 1973).

One of the most valuable and best-presented discographical works of all is *The Sousa Band: A Discography* by James R. Smart, published by the Library of Congress in Washington in 1970. Another is the set of books on Edison recordings on cylinders (1889 to 1912) by Allen Koenigsberg (Stellar Productions, New York, 1969) and *Edison Disc Recordings* by Raymond R. Wile (Eastern National Park and Monument Association, 1978). For jazz connoisseurs, the late Walter C. Allen (Stanhope, N.J.) produced *King Joe Oliver* in October 1955, later published in London by Sidgwick & Jackson. In September 1960 he produced Howard J. Waters, Jr.'s, *Jack Teagarden's Music*, and thirteen years later, *Hendersonia*, devoted to the recording and career of Fletcher Henderson, prominent black bandleader and arranger.

The continent of Europe also has its discographers of major research work. France produced Charles Delaunay in the 1930s; but in the 1950s in Berlin, Germany, Horst Lange produced a number of small books devoted to such very different musical personalities as D. J. "Nick" LaRocca, the leader and manager of the Original Dixieland Jazz Band, and

Stan Kenton, leader of one of the last of the "swing" bands of the 1940s. Lange's major work is a survey of all jazz records of any nationality issued in Germany *(Die Deutsche "78-er" Discographie der Jazz-und Hot-Dance Musik 1903-1958,* Berlin: Colloquium Verlag, 1966), and another on records of German jazz and dance music only, published by the same house also in 1966, although the discographical content of this is necessarily an appendix to a detailed narrative. In Italy, a work similar to Lange's huge volume, but concerning Italian jazz issues of all nationalities, is Giuseppe Barazzetta, Giancarlo Testoni, and Arrigo Polillo's *Enciclopedia del Jazz,* published in 1954 by Messaggerie Musicali, in Milan, while in Belgium, Robert Pernet wrote *Jazz in Little Belgium* (Brussels: Editions Sigma, 1967) and in Denmark, Jorgen Grunnet Jepsen compiled a gargantuan set of volumes totaling thousands of pages on *Jazz Records, 1942-1962* (some extending to 1965 and 1967) (Holte, Denmark: Karl Emil Knudsen, 1963-1969).

Another Belgian discography, of mammoth proportions, has recently been produced by its author, Walter Bruyninckx, of Lange Nieuwstraat 121, 2800 Mechelen. Entitled *60 Years of Recorded Jazz,* this looseleaf compilation covers jazz of all kinds in 9,000 pages, to appear twice a year, 1,500 pages at a time, in six sections, unbound, at a total cost of $234.000. It appears to be aimed at the jazz enthusiast whose concern is wholly for the sound, not for the archivist aspect, since LP details are quoted in large numbers, with only the *original* 78 issue being shown. In view of this, the value of this massive undertaking is principally for those interested mainly in postwar jazz who find Jorgen Grunnet Jepsen out of date; those concerned with pre-1942 recordings are adequately catered to already.

Perhaps the most remarkable series of discographical books to have been published in Europe at any time is the one devoted to Scandinavian recordings generally and Swedish artists and labels in particular, produced at fairly regular intervals during the 1960s and 1970s by the Nationalfonotekets in Stockholm. The Finnish Institute of Recorded Sound in Helsinki has also published valuable discographies of Finnish artists on American labels, the work of the foremost Finnish discographer, Pekka Gronow. The Swedish books include contributions from eminent authorities such as Björn Englund and Karleric Liliedahl.

The British Institute of Recorded Sound, founded in 1948 as a means of maintaining a national reference library for all kinds of recordings, as the British Museum does for books, has also published artist discographies of many kinds from time to time in its quarterly *Recorded Sound,* and various other forms of discography, sometimes by artist, sometimes by label, have appeared at irregular intervals throughout the world in a veritable jungle of specialist magazines. These usually have only a limited circulation, and as often as not are printed on duplicating paper from stencils cut with an ordinary typewriter. They may look unprofessional, but in them we can often find information on some topic of paramount importance.

The most important periodical in the United States from a discographical viewpoint is *Record Research*, published in New York more or less bi-monthly. Although its policy is to devote most of its pages to the study of jazz records and those closely akin (dance bands, blues, and so on), other forms are also covered, and since July 1961, the entire master list of recordings made by the Plaza Music Company (subsequently the American Record Corporation and later still CBS) has been appearing in serial form, presented by one of America's greatest discographers, Carl Kendziora. Britain's two principal discographical magazines are *Storyville* (already referred to as being devoted solely to jazz, and with a fairly obvious bias toward early black jazz) and *The Record Collector*, published bi-monthly as the others, by J. F. E. Dennis of Ipswich, Suffolk. This, like *Storyville*, is set up in lithographs and on glossy paper. Its policy is concerned solely with operatic and concert singers, almost exclusively of the past, as the name may suggest.

As might be expected, the earliest attempts at discography, or "listings" as we have seen they were known, were sketchy, being little more than slightly expanded extracts from a sequence of catalog entries. Dates were very rarely given more closely than the year of recording, if at all, and then apparently guessed at or deduced from the dates on the covers of the catalogs that were the principal source of supply of such information. We shall be examining these and other sources of information in the next chapter.

The location of a recording session was usually given if the subject of the discography was a serious artist. Neither Delaunay nor Schleman concerned themselves with details of this sort. Original and some subsequent catalog numbers were always given, but matrix numbers rarely appeared, and as a rule details of different takes were alluded to in footnotes that simply remarked that two or more performances by an artist of certain titles were known to have been issued. Here again, this applies mostly to operatic and vocal discographies; until Orin Blackstone's and Albert McCarthy's individual works were published, jazz discographies made little or no reference to the many examples of differing performances that had been made available simultaneously with the first issue, or subsequent to it. This is strange, as improvised jazz provides more obvious differences in performance than a reading from a score, although there are many occasions in the history of operatic records when two or more takes of an aria by a famous singer have been issued, with very easily discernible differences.

To the late Walter C. Allen must go the credit for instituting the accepted method of presentation for a jazz discography, be it of one artist or a group. A sketchy outline, distilled from catalogs, has not been accepted since he produced the monography of "King" Joe Oliver, the black cornet player. Personnels as complete as human endeavor and research can make them, or at least the full details of instrumentation of a band, are as always de rigeur, but now, matrix numbers, take numbers or digits, exact titles (and composers exactly as shown on the labels of the records, even if misspelled), all issue numbers, and variations on artist credits between issues must be included in any discography of an individual artist or group of artists. Jazz records generally appeal to those to whom the composer of the original melody is of little consequence, thus in an all-embracing discographical encyclopedia, it is not necessarily regarded as an essential feature; but in a work devoted to serious music in any form, the composer or composers and, where known, arrangers are as much a part of the discography as the title or any of the numerical details. The same applies to discographies of ragtime music, for although this was the forerunner of jazz in popular esteem in the twentieth century, and forms to a great extent the basis of jazz, it should be played as written by the composer according to his explicit instructions, exactly as a Chopin prelude or a Brahms intermezzo. It follows that in a discography of ragtime music, the composer is all-important, perhaps more so than the performer, since most recordings of ragtime made during the first quarter or so of this century were not *by* the composer, they remain our nearest link *with* the composer, although they were probably recorded by musicians who were competent to play anything set in front of them by an artists' manager, and not of any particular significance in themselves.

It is strange that a detailed and accurately dated discography of opera and concert singers has yet to be produced, since these were the subject of the first book length work deserving of the title "discography," as we have seen. Such a work is now (1979) in preparation; it is fair, however, to note that the individual discographies of this soprano or that baritone, published over the last quarter of a century or more in *The Record Collector* do show the material in a much more academically acceptable, detailed form than will be found in any of the editions of Roberto Bauer's book.

One noticeable major difference between the presentation of a discography of a serious work, composer, or artist (other than singers) and that of jazz and the more popular forms is that whereas the majority of the latter are listed chronologically, the tendency of the former is toward alphabetical listing by title. The individual major discographies of all kinds will be discussed at length and in detail in chapter 4.

With the establishing of vast national collections of records of all kinds, from wax cylinders of the 1890s through 78 rpm discs to long-playing microgrooved vinylite pressings, tapes, cassettes, and even film sound-tracks, not only in the United States and Great Britain, but in various European countries and Australia, an awareness now exists on an official level that a discography is not just a form of musical bookkeeping but a valid and valuable account of events in cultural (and often political) life of the last eighty or ninety years. The discographer, that philatelic eccentric, begins to take his place as an historian whose work is of comparable importance to that of Samuel Pepys in the seventeeth century or James Boswell in the eighteenth. His insistence on the excavation of relics of the past, whether of singing, playing, or speaking, in any selected form or idiom is surely akin to the dedication of the archaeologists whose tireless work in the Middle East and elsewhere has shown us the civilizations of Minos, Egypt, Sumeria, India, China. . . . Much remains to be done. How it has been done and can still be done will be discussed in the following chapter.

3

The Creation
of a Discography

AS WITH any worthwhile project, the preparation of a discography of any kind necessarily involves a great deal of research, checking, and cross-checking, and frequently backtracking as new and sometimes conflicting evidence comes to light. The recording industry as a commercial entity has only existed for a matter of eighty years or so at this writing, and thus much of its life is within the living memory of many senior citizens. However, because so little of value was written concerning its activites *at the time* of its earliest days other than entries in catalogs, unearthing detailed information on what was recorded, by whom, when, and where becomes as daunting as if it were contemporary with King Tutankhamen.

The starting point for any discography must be, of course, a combination of at least some of the records themselves, and the publicity material announcing them to the public as new additions to the manufacturer's catalog. It might seem to be a simple matter to acquire a set of catalogs of the company or companies known to have recorded the subject of the discography, but because human nature is what it is, and the catalogs of yesterday (that is, pre-LP, even prewar) cost little or usually nothing at all, those who possessed these catalogs to determine what records had been made of their favorite music tended to destroy them as out-of-date waste paper once a new edition had been published. Paper salvage drives during World War II contributed largely to this sad state of affairs. The monthly leaflets—usually known as supplements in the trade and among collectors—listing the newest additions to the catalog were usually regarded as of even less consequence, and tossed aside accordingly. Some enthusiasts, however, perhaps with a lesser sense of patriotism at the time of the salvage drive, or at least a greater perception of their possible future use, did preserve these flimsy booklets, some even taking the trouble to have the more comprehensive and informative of them bound like magazines.

It has been well said, however, that frequently the old catalogs and supplements are more valuable than most of the records they list. Because of their more or less ephemeral nature, or what was regarded as such by those who acquired them casually while making a purchase in a record store, it is quite understandable that they would be looked on as dispensable within a matter of a few weeks or at most a year or so. There is another and somewhat more permanent, though not much less rare source of information about records as they were issued: the music magazines and those designed for phonograph/gramophone/record-player owners. Less so now, but frequently during the first half of the century, these periodicals regularly published dated listings of the latest records, sometimes an exact copy of the manufacturers' publicity material. Even when there were no advertisements showing what the latest issues were, these would often be discussed by the critics on the staff of the magazine, complete with details of artists, titles, and catalog numbers.

A very valuable source of information on records when annual catalogs and monthly supplements are almost impossible to find is the symposia of these, reprinted in full, in the issues of the American *Phonograph and Talking Machine Weekly*, the monthly *Talking Machine Journal* and *Talking Machine World*, and the British *Phono Trader, Phono Record, Sound Wave, Talking Machine News*, and, of course, *Gramophone*. These can usually be found complete and bound in the major public libraries; very occasionally, single copies or even annual volumes can be picked up in bookshops, secondhand stores, and auction rooms. (I am considering American and British magazines for the purpose of these notes, but no doubt much the same situation exists in other countries.)

One of the most remarkable guides to sources of information for the compilation of a discography of almost any kind is contained in the *Association for Recorded Sound Collections Journal*, Vol. X, No. 1 (1979). This is the work of Gary-Gabriel Gisondi, and lists no fewer than 126 periodicals, all of which are known to offer valuable material for the purpose. Admittedly, not all of them are currently available (the house magazines of the Victor Talking Machine Company and the Gramophone Company, reaching back well over sixty years, are very rare and valuable collectors' prizes in themselves, of course), but as a stepping-off point for any discographical research, this listing is indispensable.

It would be wise to reflect, however, that manufacturers' lists, catalogs, or any kind of publicity material, though most valuable as a starting point for a discography, should not be regarded as infallible. As a discographer, I can quote many examples of records that were made, tested, accepted, allocated reference numbers, announced for sale, and advised to the trade and which for some reason enjoyed—if that is the word—a very brief life on the market. So brief, in fact, was that life in some cases that it never received a mention in any of the normal publicity outlets. A record could be announced immediately after the cut-off date for one catalog and then, because of poor sales, some inherent defect that could not be remedied easily, or even in some cases the insistence of the artist concerned, be withdrawn from circulation before the next edition of the catalog. One British dance record was given a catalog number by the company that made it and, for no reason that can now be determined, was cancelled at the very last moment before issue. Exactly a year later, equipped with a completely different number, it was again announced, and again it was cancelled—but this time not quite so rapidly. One large concern, accustomed to receiving a standing order of three copies of everything issued by all the major companies, in fact secured three copies of this particular record. Thus, to this day, nearly half a century later, this concern is the custodian of the only copies known to exist of what must be one of the rarest records in history. The fact that it is of considerable appeal as a "hot" jazz record makes it of interest not only to those who specialize in dance music, but also of course to jazz connoisseurs.

Having established at least a framework of what records were made of a given artist *and issued*, by reference to the publicity material and contemporary reviews in the musical press, the next step is to track down a copy of each of the records and note all the numerical details shown on it. This is a fascinating and culturally, even emotionally, satisfying undertaking, because acquisition of the records, even on a temporary basis, invariably means playing them and largely enjoying the performances on them. What, though, if there are gaps in the continuity of the numbers, suggesting titles by the same artist that were never issued, perhaps for some reason never considered for issue beyond the point where a test record was made and failed? Discussion with other collectors and authorities can often reveal a fragment of the missing information, but often there are gaps that obstinately refuse to be filled.

Here, the only course is to seek access to the original recording files of the company or companies that made the records originally. Naturally, these files are the private property of the companies, and it can be readily understood that they may not always be inclined to detail members of their staff to make copies of the relevant items of missing information. Such a procedure can be time-consuming and, as a result, costly. In the main, however, the major companies in both the United States and Britain are very cooperative in these matters, and RCA and CBS in America, and EMI and Decca in England have always been most willing to allow me personal access to their files. I cannot write too glowingly of the welcome and hospitality they all accorded me when I visited their various head offices, intent on solving as many strange mysteries as I could.

As I remarked earlier, however, while RCA in New York and Decca in England have maintained magnificently complete written records, certain earlier (pre-1910) Columbia recording files no longer exist, and little remains of the ledgers and index cards of the General Phonograph Company, producers of OKeh records until absorbed by Columbia in November 1926. CBS has fallen heir to the files of the American Record Corporation, and from the summer of 1927, the ledgers and cards referring to the records made by and for the corporation and *its* predecessor, the Plaza Music Company, are intact. For details of recordings made prior to this date, however, we have to refer to the serialized listing in *Record Research* which I mentioned in chapter 2. Even this, despite the long and valiant efforts of compiler Carl Kendziora, is by no means complete, and unless every individual side that was allocated a number was actually issued, many of its blanks must inevitably remain so. For the pre-Columbian OKeh material, all that can be done here once the surviving details have been noted is to reconstruct the files by noting fully everything encountered that bears an OKeh label or that of one of its subsidiaries in Europe. I have been engaged in just such a reconstruction since 1942, and I think I may be perhaps 40 percent complete.

Similarly, I have attempted to reconstruct those sections of the Columbia files that no longer exist in the original form. I have been surpassed in this, however, by the superb enterprise of two American discographers, Bill Bryant and Tim Brooks, who have examined hundreds of Columbia records of all kinds made prior to November 4, 1910, the date of the earliest listed item in the CBS files, including the various subsidiary labels on which these pioneer sides appeared.

In view of the enormously valuable material of a jazz, blues, and Afro-American nature issued by the mid-West Paramount label between 1920 and 1932, enthusiasts for music of this kind have hoped for many years that someday, somewhere, someone would find the original files that could tell so much about the artists and their recordings, which once were featured so richly in the Paramount catalog. Rumor persisted that when the company went out of existence in the Depression, its files were passed into the hands of one of its impresarios, but he has denied this. No documents concerning the activities of the Cameo Record Corporation of New York, Orlando R. Marsh's Autograph label of Chicago, or the earliest three years of the Brunswick Balke Collender Company and the Aeolian Vocalion Company have ever been found, either; MCA in Universal City, California, holds the Decca files and the ragged, incomplete remnants of the Brunswick and Vocalion ledgers, but the whereabouts of the rest remains a mystery. Dealing with artists who recorded for these companies is thus a matter of finding all the issued records and noting all that they can tell us—until and unless, by some incredible stroke of fortune, the original files are found.

As it happens, such strokes of fortune are not unthinkable or unknown by any means. In the winter of 1952, George W. Kay, then living in Rushville, Indiana, gained access to the entire range of files and index cards of the Starr Piano Company of Richmond, Indiana, which from 1916 to 1930 had produced the Gennett label and from 1925 to 1934 the Champion, and with these files he acquired a wealth of extremely valuable jazz and blues material. Nor are such miracles confined to the United States; in the summer of 1962, while some workmen were reconstructing one of the studios in the Decca building in West Hampstead, London, they found walled up a number of faded and ragged handwritten ledgers that had been the property of the Crystalate Company, absorbed by Decca twenty-five years before. At one blow, all the recordings made for the Victory, Eclipse, Crown, and Imperial labels, together with six-inch "nursery" records issued as Mimosa and Marspen, were made known to us. A collection of cards was revealed as the only known documents relative to the products of the Duophone Syndicate, once a subsidiary of British Brunswick Ltd., which itself had been absorbed by Decca. Strangely, nothing has apparently survived of the ledgers and files of Metropole Records, or any of the English branch of Vocalion, or of Crystalate's last thriving label, Rex. Nor does Decca have anything pertaining to Edison Bell's recordings other than those the Decca company itself recorded for Edison Bell Winner after buying the name and the firm's assets in January 1933. In this connection, it is of perhaps rather melancholy interest that early in 1960, while browsing in a dusty secondhand bookstore in a rather seedy district of London, I found a ledger that listed all the *twelve-inch* Edison Bell records in fullest possible detail. At that time I was only concerned with jazz in its more or less "pure" sense, and as there was nothing of the sort in the ledger, and not nearly enough spare cash in my pocket, I declined to buy it. I cannot count the number of times since that I have reviled myself for being so incredibly short-sighted and lacking in initiative. A few weeks earlier, I had been invited to buy anything I needed from the effects of the late J. E. Hough, proprietor of Edison Bell, Ltd. I often wonder if that ledger I saw had been thrown out by Mr. Hough's family, and with it, perhaps, a similar one or more, covering Edison Bell's ten- and eight-inch labels, and, if so, where they eventually came to rest.

Yet another incident whereby a valuable discographical document was rescued from oblivion with perhaps only hours, even minutes to spare, is the case of the original ledger of the British Homophone Company, Ltd.,

who produced Sterno records from 1926 to 1935, along with various subsidiary labels. Long believed to be lost forever, probably destroyed, the
tattered book was discovered in an ashcan awaiting collection by the
garbage men on the very day a British collector happened to be visiting
the British Homophone factory. He acquired the precious piece of "garbage"
and is preserving it for posterity, with the blessing of British Homophone,
no longer engaged in the production of records on the commerical market.

Some years ago, I attempted to discover the whereabouts of the Pathé
recording files. The original Pathé Frères Pathéphone Company in London
had been sold to Columbia at the end of December 1928, but not a vestige
of these files remained as far as I could discover. Next, I tried CBS in
New York, with the same result. There seemed only one possible chance
of success, namely that Pathé-Marconi in Paris might have retained the
lost documents. Alas, in a charming letter one the executives explained
that her firm did have these files until the Nazi occupation; they were
destroyed as waste paper by order of the commander of the occupying
forces.

The indefatigable Carl Kendziora again has produced a most valuable
booklet on the Perfect label, from 1922 to 1930 a Pathé subsidiary, showing details of almost all the records issued in the Dance Music series with
composer-credit, numbers of all kinds, as many dates as could be traced,
and much valuable information on the history of the label, all by examining at least one copy of every Perfect record issued in those years. The
unissued sides must remain a matter for eternal conjecture, however.

Presumably the same fate was meted out to any documents regarding
European recordings by Pathé, which as a company has a history reaching back to the late 1890s. \

When it is necessary to ascertain the personnel of a band or orchestra,
or a small instrumental group (perhaps accompanying a popular singer),
the original ledgers sometimes provide the answers, occasionally with
surprising results. Since 1936, it seems that the names of members of
the American Federation of Musicians were required by law to be entered,
and as a result, a perusal of the RCA Victor and Bluebird files will usually
show these details, as will those of CBS and Decca. No such requirement
seems to have obtained in Britain, for although there is evidence that
some orchestras were analyzed on paper, this does not seem to have been
a general rule; at all events, when my own band made a session for Parlophone in London in 1958, we were not called on to provide our identities
in writing. It way be that there are held at the headquarters of the AFM
documents showing which of its members appeared on whose make of
records on dates prior to 1936, but hitherto, there has been no cooperation
from the Federation.

It has been suggested that the music publishers' copyright records might prove fruitful of information concerning recording dates, but although most of them can and do divulge the titles, composers, and artists as well as the companies, they cannot necessarily show the numbers of the records, and certainly not the actual dates of recording. They may say when a number for recording was released, and presumably no record of it could have been made prior to that date, but that much can usually be assessed by comparison between the known date of the same title by a make whose files exist and the probable date, or date of issue, of the one where they do not.

Knowing the exact date of issue of a record can at least be of some help in establishing its date of recording, of course. This can be assimilated into the reconstruction of the recording ledgers, and if the aspiring discographer is fortunate enough to find a test pressing of some recording made by a company whose files no longer exist, he may find that it bears the date on its plain label, or etched into the surface of the disc itself, either under the label and showing through it or around the outer rim. (American Columbia in early times adopted the latter procedure and the rare occasions when an eleven-inch disc containing a ten-inch performance, so to speak, shows up in some junkyard, it will be seen to have full discographical details handwritten on the extra surface area, which would have been removed during the finished pressings.)

Records manufactured in the Pathé Frères Pathéphone factory in the London suburb of Stonebridge Park invariably bear a date which is not the recording date. I interviewed the retired engineer whose job it was to scratch the *date of processing the master* on the run-off area; as a result it comes out mirror-fashion. It bears not even a slightly useful relationship to the recording date, and discographers noticing it on such labels as Actuelle, Brunswick Cliftophone, Ideal Scala, Perfect, and even Sterno of 1929 vintage should disregard it.

Perhaps the most interesting method of preparing a discography of an artist is to interview the artist himself or herself, or, if in the nature of things that is no longer possible, some relative or even a close friend can sometimes be of assistance. Happy indeed is the discographer who finds that the object of his attention kept an engagement book, and when I say "kept," I mean that literally, in the sense of retaining it. The great Finnish-American trumpet-player Sylvester Ahola, who worked in London between the end of 1927 and the summer of 1931, maintained and retained such a book, entering all kinds of useful, even vital scraps of information on his many recording dates during that time, such as the exact location of the studio of the company named, and notes on the personnel of the band in a number of instances. His generosity and patience in handing over the relevant details has been my only source of accurate information on many obscure recording companies' activities. Similarly, I am indebted to the nephew of the late Nat Star, a British clarinet and saxophone player who worked as a session man and as the coordinator of dozens of recording bands for almost every company in London, large and small alike. The young man knew little of his uncle's activities half a century ago, but he willingly lent me some diaries he found among his late relative's papers— which at once filled in a number of gaps in my general knowledge of the dance band world of those days.

While interviewing the actual musicians or singers has its delightful moments, as most of them are or were delightful people, it can also have its drawbacks and its frustrations. The great German operatic soprano Erika Wedekind, who was known by Bauer to have made some seventeen titles for the Gramophone and Typewriter Company and its successor the Gramophone Company apparently in Dresden between 1906 and 1908, produced her engagement book not long before she died. In it she had entered the fact that she had undertaken seven recording sessions, not the three attributed to her by Bauer, and that these took place in Berlin, between the summer of 1905 and the opening weeks of 1910!

Such a discovery, of course, is of immense importance where the original company evidence no longer exists. We may be forgiven for wondering how many other great artists of any kind kept diaries or other written evidence of their recording activities, how many of them retained them until their deaths, and how many of the kith and kin have recognized them for what they are and treasured them accordingly. Nick LaRocca, composer of *Tiger Rag* and many other jazz standards, bequeathed his engagement books, files, photographs, and other documents to the Jazz Archives of Tulane University; without them, we should have no idea of the exact date of recording of the extremely rare titles the Original Dixieland Jazz Band made for Aeolian in 1917, or the slightly less rare items recorded in London for the Columbia Graphophone Company. Little remains of the original files of the latter and nothing at all of the former.

Frustrating as it may be to know that Erika Wedekind recorded more titles than she has been given credit for without knowing what they were (she did not list them in her diary), it can be even more so when a musician or a singer in the course of an interview recalls a studio session at which he or she recorded a title or even a series of titles of which nothing more is known. Memory is a very fallible thing, as we all know. Some musicians have almost total recall, even after half a century, while others have only the most shadowy recollections of what they recorded, where, when, for what company, and with whom, even after perhaps only half that time or less. Sometimes an incident in the outside world that occurred on the day of the session will pinpoint the date ("I remember we made that on the day Babe Ruth hit sixty home runs"), and if the studio was that of a company whose files can be checked, another small shred of evidence can be fitted into the discographical jigsaw. If, on the other hand, the mysterious record was made for a defunct company of whose exact activities we know little, such information can provide the starting point for putting at least fairly accurate dates to sessions by others which, judging by their numbers, must be quite near in time to the one remembered by our subject—if we can find it!

One British dance band musician recalled having made a record of a tune that his regular employer did not seem to have made. He was most insistent, so I admit I decided privately that it must have been recorded as a balance test without any thought of issue. Years later it transpired that the entire band had played hookey, as it were, from their contracted company's studio, and made for a rival firm not just the title recalled by the man I was interviewing, but five others—all of which were issued under the most improbable pseudonyms! Rare though they are, I located copies of all of them, and having tuned my ear to the distinctive sound of the principal soloists in the band, as well as the overall ensemble sound, I was able to verify that my subject's memory was completely and fault-lessly accurate, over thirty years later.

Strangely, perhaps, in view of the length of time that has elapsed since they were made, the easiest records to date exactly are the the seven-inch single-sided pioneering products of Emile Berliner in the 1890s. The reason is simply that with Teutonic thoroughness, Berliner decided that the recording date should be entered *on the record itself,* and so in the majority of examples still in existence, we can see this very important feature. Sometimes it is in the form of a die-stamp, etched into the surface of the smooth central area where the label would be on a more modern record; more often, and in particular on British and other European Berliner records, it is handwritten, sometimes American style (2-8-99 for February 8, 1899), more often British (8-2-99 for the same date). The importance of this can hardly be exaggerated, for it means that even if the matrix number is illegible, only partly visible, or completely omitted (all these conditions occur on Berliners), we can still assess at once the position of the record in a discography of the artist or type of music. There were few singers of importance who condescended to make records for Berliner, but there are numerous examples of early ragtime music in the Berliner catalogs, played by bands, orchestras, and banjoists (not, alas, by the great ragtime composers themselves, as the piano was one of the most difficult of instruments to record satisfactorily in the earliest days). In the British catalogs, also, there are many specimens of the art of the great music hall and musical stage artists of the turn of the century, who cheer-fully agreed to take part in what must have seemed something of an interesting experiment.

The historian in the world of song who sets out to compile a discography of an imporatant artist inevitably has problems, usually concerned with tracking down copies of the records in order to obtain details of type of label, numerical data, exact title, composer and artist credits, and possibly accompaniment.

It is common for a vocal record to show no details of accompaniment —piano on most of the earliest items, orchestra of a kind on the majority of the later ones. As often as not, the pianist is not named, nor the conductor of the orchestra, and examples can be found of a label indicating the accompaniment is by orchestra when in fact it is by a piano, and vice versa. On at least two of Fernando de Lucia's records, made in 1909, the labels show accompaniments completely at variance with what can be heard on the records themselves: an "orchestra" becomes a trio of violin, guitar, and mandolin, and "violin and piano" are transmuted into clarinet, flute, and what sounds like a harmonium. These are further examples of why it is inadvisable to put blind faith in label information!

Having surmounted the more general problems, and documented the entire output of his chosen artist, with as much of the customary detail as he can obtain, the vocalist discographer has few if any further difficulties as a rule. The same applies to preparing a discography of artists of the stage, screen, and radio, as they seldom present problems of identification. How could they? Their very stardom was the principal selling point of their records, and as one cynic put it, when discussing the popularity of a vocalist: "They'd buy his records if he sang a railroad timetable as long as his name was on the label and he was actually singing!" The jazz, blues, and dance band discographer, on the other hand, is at once and permanently confronted with problems of identification, not only of the soloists (instruments and/or vocal), but of the entire band, frequently of the number of each type of instrument, and even of the instruments themselves.

This kind of problem happens with popular artists and blues singers, too. What is named on the label is not necessarily what is heard coming from the speaker. When the late Jimmie Rodgers's "Blue Yodel No. 9" was issued in England, it was said to be accompanied by "guitars and string bass," but, in fact, all that can be heard are Louis Armstrong playing trumpet and his wife, Lil, at the piano. The label for the other side, "Jimmie the Kid," allegedly accompanied by orchestra, is perhaps nearer the truth in that the supporting instruments are two violins, two guitars, and one string bass.

Identification of the instruments visible through the studio control panel seems to have caused a certain amount of difficulty on occasion. One Chicago session, held in the ballroom of the Webster Hotel by the old Victor Talking Machine Company, featured New Orleans pianist Jelly-Roll Morton and his Red Hot Peppers. This was a jazz band with classic instrumentation, but according to the recording ledger, two cornets were used. At no time on any of the three titles made and issued can these be heard; one is very much in evidence, but never two. A possible explanation submitted itself when it was realized that the street noises on one of the titles, introduced to bring a touch of realism to the proceedings, included a klaxon horn wielded by a white visitor to the studios. For more than twenty years, discographers all over the world offered all kinds of suggestions as to the identity of the second cornet. The favorite was one Lee Collins, who did indeed take part in a Morton recording of the same number, but without the street noises, for Autograph records, and just two years earlier.

At times, Duke Ellington's clarinet player was credited with playing a flute, and when Duke Ellington introduced a valve-trombone into his brass section, it was entered in the Victor files as a French horn.

All who have ever attempted a discography of a jazz musician or a band will be familiar with the pitfalls attending the identification by sound of a soloist or ensemble player. Not only is an accurate ear for turns of phrase, vibrato, and general placing of notes for a wide range of musicians on many instruments necessary, but a knowledge of the geographical whereabouts of the more outstanding musicians is also essential; if a certain trombonist, let us say, was undoubtedly in Chicago when a record, whose sound suggests he was present, is known to have been made in New York, it is obvious that some other trombonist in New York was attempting to sound like that musician.

Determining the location of a musician at a given date is one of the most difficult assignments for a jazz or dance music discographer. Memories of the musicians themselves can help—or they can hinder. The best sources of reliable information on these points are the periodicals for the profession and those interested in it published *at the time.* American magazines such as *Variety* and *Billboard* have often been of service, but more frequently the long-established *Metronome* and the tabloid *Down Beat,* introduced in 1934, have been profitably consulted by jazz and dance band researchers. It is enouraging to find details on these matters in the magazines designed for the record trade: the *Talking Machine World* is particularly helpful, frequently illustrating its pages during the 1920s with photographs of bands actually engaged in recording, from which it is possible, with a working knowledge of what certain musicians looked like as well as how they sounded, to pick out at least some of the personnel and thus verify their presence in whatever location is named in the news item.

In Britain, one periodical stands out above all others as a reliable source of information on what was happening in the jazz and dance band world, on both sides of the Atlantic: the *Melody Maker,* first published in January 1926 and still very much in circulation. The record reviews are sometimes inclined to make curiously misleading comments as to the supposed identities of some musicians, but details found in the newsletter from the New York correspondents, and in instructive articles by "star" dance band musicians are very helpful, when the authors name their colleagues on what were then recent recording sessions.

Perhaps the simplest discographical research is into the world of the cinema or pipe organ. Once enormously popular in every sense of the word, recordings of these instruments have long since dwindled to virtually nothing, as incidental music in film theaters relied more and more on long-playing records and tapes. In their heyday, during the late 1920s, throughout the 1930s, and perhaps a little way into the 1940s, all the most palatial movie theaters in the United States and Great Britain installed a pipe organ. This was usually manufactured by the firm of Wurlitzer, and recordings of popular songs and light classics played on these vast instruments ("the mighty Wurlitzer" was the most common description) fairly rolled off the presses on both sides of the Atlantic. Since their virtual demise, many nostalgiacs with the taste, the space, and the money have bought up the original organs and installed them in their own homes, rather than see them go to the scrap merchants; others less wealthy and with much less space collect the records made by the great exponents of the theater organ. As no other musicians were usually present when recordings were made in the theaters and recording studios equipped with pipe organs, no research is needed to determine personnel (although a very few feature a solo violin, occasionally a xylophone, vibraphone, or other percussion), and the location of the recording is usually stated on the labels. Just as jazz connoisseurs can distinguish their favorite soloists, so can the theater organ enthusiasts, and many can detect subtle differences between the register of the organ in one theater and that in another.

The problems facing discographers of country-style music and of blues are similar to those confronting the jazz and dance band discographers, although perhaps on a smaller scale. This is mainly because most country-and-Western artists, and "hillbilly" bands, consist of only a few artists, mostly playing stringed instruments. Occasionally there might be a clarinet, a saxophone, a piano, more frequently a harmonica, and/or a jews-harp, but the basic form of a country-style band is a violin or two, some guitars, banjos and the like, string bass, and sometimes percussion. These are often played by the singers themselves, who have a helpful habit of encouraging each other by name, thereby helping to solve some problems relating to personnel.

In the case of Negro blues recordings, the problems of identifying accompanists are still smaller, as a considerable number of them are field recordings by self-accompanied singers on guitar or piano; often the identities of any other accompanists are shown on the recording ledgers or cards, if not on the labels of the records themselves. (In this connection, the General Phonograph Corporation was particularly helpful, their OKeh labels crediting the accompanists by name and instrument even if there were three of them, almost as if they anticipated the intense interest that future generations would show in their superb products.) Here again, the uninhibited style of performance frequently allowed the blues singer to apostrophize his (or more usually her) accompanists by name. Here, also, we find a degree of frustration when the singer addresses the accompanists by some sobriquet meaning nothing to anyone but the soloist and the musician themselves.

These sources of information, with all their strengths and weaknesses, are the most obvious fields of research when planning and compiling a modern, scientific discography. There are perhaps a few others. The dating of a desired record can sometimes be achieved by a reference in the popular press to a recording session by some unimportant artist, the products of which are known to be numbered very closely to the subject of the research. An example of this is the occasion when a popular Irish variety artist sang his latest success to a delighted throng of office workers and passers-by from a window above a London street during lunch break, and promptly went on to the Edison Bell studios to record the same song. The record of this is of no interest as jazz, dance music, serious music, or historical speech, of course, but it is neatly numbered between two sessions by the visiting Southern Rag-a-Jazz Band from Carolina, thereby dating both much more accurately than would otherwise be possible. Another Edison Bell date can be fixed by a news item reporting that H.R.H. the Prince of Wales (later King Edward VIII and subsequently the Duke of Windsor) had heard the black American band, The Versatile Three, play and sing a number called *You Know What I Mean*, and was so impressed by it, he asked for an advance copy to be sent to him in time for it to go with him on one of his world tours. "This was recorded and a copy sent to His Royal Highness a few days ago," said the report, "and he sails today."

These notes will serve to illustrate how assiduous a discographer must be, if a maximum degree of accuracy is to be achieved. Our next step will be to consider the major types of discographies, their forms of arrangement and content, and their comparative strengths and weaknesses.

4

Major Types
of Discography

FOR THE purposes of this chapter, it is best that the various types of disco-graphy be considered quite separately, for as we have seen, the needs of one or two of them are quite different from those of the rest.

A truly detailed, comprehensive discography of serious works does not yet seem to exist. Using the composers as the point of departure, so to speak, we have, of course, the *World Encyclopaedia of Recorded Music*, which is an admirable reference if all that is required is an answer to a question such as "Has there ever been a recording of such-and-such a symphony, string quartet or song-cycle?" or "Has this or that concert overture been recorded by one particular orchestra?" It does not set out the matrix number, take number or digit, location, or recording date of any of the myriad of entries, arranged under the composer's name in no apparent order of recording or even of issue. While it may be felt that detail of this sort is unnecessary in a work of this kind, that the date of *composition* is of primary importance, it is nevertheless useful, even sometimes essential, to have at least some idea of the date of recording. A compiler of a program of the recorded works of, let us say, Francis Poulenc, needs to know the date of recording of pieces played by the composer himself, if only to obtain information about the probable quality of the recording.

Discographies of conductors, to the best of my knowledge, mainly exist in articles scattered throughout music magazines of the civilized world, or as appendices to books devoted to their careers on the concert platform. One admirable exception to this is Jerrold Moore's *Elgar on Record: The Composer and the Gramophone* (London: Hamish Hamilton, 1975). Here the fullest details of the entire products of the recording sessions at which Sir Edward Elgar conducted are given, from immediately prior to World War I until just before his death exactly twenty years later. We have the name of the orchestra, the location of the studio, the matrix numbers, and take letters or digits relative to each work or section of work, and all the labels on which the sides were issued, up to the time of going to press. For the curiosity-hunters, there are also details of some piano improvisations recorded by the composer-conductor himself in 1929; it goes without saying that the exact date of each session is included.

There are a number of small booklets, ranging in size from eighteen pages to seventy-seven, devoted to the discographies of such conductors as Sir Thomas Beecham (Redondo Beach, Calif.: The Sir Thomas Beecham Society, 1970) and the works of Henning Smidth Olsen on Edwin Fischer and Wilhelm Furtwängler, Sir Dan Godfrey, and the Bournemouth Municipal Orchestra. The latter has been covered by Stuart Upton (Purley, Surrey, England: The Mascotte Society, 1970) and the Vintage Light Music Society (West Wickham, England: 1979).

As with any first-class discography on any aspect of recorded sound, the presentation is in chronological order. The standard work on early singers by Robert Bauer (see chapter 3) differs, and rightly, from the occasional articles in *The Gramophone* and elsewhere, in that each singer is listed by Bauer alphabetically and his or her records follow in at least approximate chronological order. The compilers of the individual articles list everything by title, alphabetically, as in the case of the Melba listing by Henry McK. Rothermel, showing the catalog numbers (but no matrix numbers or take details), in a rather jumbled fashion, the location, but only the year of recording, and, again with Melba, a curious collection of code letters referring to a list of twenty-four footnotes showing whether a title was electrically recorded, accompanied by piano or orchestra, the price of the original single-sided issue, and even an arbitrary comment on the quality of the record itself. The "listing" of Emmy Destinn's records merely shows their catalog numbers and titles, with few composers, virtually no dates of even the most approximate nature, and no matrix numbers. A sort of discography of Enrico Caruso's records is included in the account of his last years by his widow, Dorothy Caruso (*Enrico Caruso: His Life and Death*. New York: Simon & Schuster, 1945). It is by Jack Caidin of the Collectors Record Shop in New York, and is also presented in alphabetical order of title. It shows no matrix numbers, take details, or locations, but it does give the original catalog number and subsequent numbers. Dates are given to a month; accompaniments are shown only if they are by other than an orchestra.

By far the most detailed and professional discography of Caruso is the work of John Richard Bolig. This eighty-eight-page book (hardcover) was published by the Eldridge Reeve Johnson Museum in Dover, Delaware, in 1973, and it lists every Caruso record chronologically, as an acceptable discography should, with an alphabetical index of titles, accompanists, and other artists who sang on records with the great tenor. If the method and presentation of this book were applied to all discographies, at least of great singers, what a very happy state collectors and students of their work would enjoy!

Bauer, on the other hand, despite his listing titles made by each singer in chronological order, omits almost all matrix numbers and thus take details, and the only reissue numbers shown are such as the European catalog number of a title originally recorded by Victor in the United States, or vice versa. Double-sided issues are not referred to at all. He groups titles together under a single year as a rule, and makes no attempt to differentiate between the various sessions that were held in that year. At the time of publication of the original *Historical Records,* this was evidently quite sufficient; nine years later, P. G. Hurst's *The Golden Age Recorded* adopted the same format. This is perhaps not surprising, as Hurst was notoriously opposed to any record that was not an original pressing, or at least one that did not bear the same outward appearance as the original (catalog number, matrix number, and so on). Repressings from the original masters merited only disdain; dubbings from original pressings were to him fakes, almost forgeries, to be eschewed at all costs. Considering the quality of most pre-1960 dubbings, even when produced by a major company, there is something to be said for this attitude toward them, but nevertheless, in a *complete* discography of great singers, or any other artists, such "fakes" should be given a place.

A booklet devoted to the records of John McCormack was published in 1972 by the Oakwood Press, Surrey, England. This is the work of L. F. MacDermott Roe, and although it lists McCormack's records by title alphabetically, it does so with a thoroughness that is quite unknown in any other booklength discography of a singer. All the essential details are shown, except locations, strangely; it is rather a pity that the unissued Victor and "His Master's Voice" titles are listed in a separate section at the back, but generally this is a model discography of its kind.

The Sousa book referred to in chapter 2 also lists the titles alphabetically, dividing them into sections according to whether they are cylinders, Berliner, or Victor discs. There is also a chronological section devoted to the Victors only.

Reverting for a moment to the discographies of vocalists, there are two popular singers who have each had discographies published: Bing Crosby and Al Bowlly. Both are presented in the now customary form of chronological order of session, with all details except composers shown. (The Al Bowlly discography is my own and is designed to include only the details of 78 rpm recordings and issues. Such is the enormous worldwide popularity of Al Bowlly, who was a victim of the air raids on London in 1941, that long-playing records of his 78s are continually being issued on various labels. I decided to omit these as a matter of policy, wishing to make the discography complete within certain limits. Because of the influx of LPs on such a scale, absolute completeness would be impossible.)

I have also authored *The Complete Entertainment Discography* (New York: Arlington House, 1973) and two books published in London by General Gramophone Publications Ltd., *London Musical Shows on Record, 1897-1976* (1978) and *British Music Hall on Record* (1979) set out the work of each artist strictly chronologically, or as nearly so as years of research along the lines indicated in chapter 3 could make them, each session headed with the location and date. The matrix number and take letter or digit are included in the left-hand column, then the title as shown on the label or in the recording files, and in a column on the right the make and number of each known issue. I use the word "rejected" to denote any title not issued on a 78 rpm record, as this is an accurate description of its status; as far as issue in this, the original, form is concerned, it must be counted as rejected rather than merely "unissued," the term used by some discographers. Some performances, recorded at 78 rpm when this was the standard speed, but never issued in that form, have found their way on to the market as entries in various long-playing albums, and I have done my best to include these with their LP numbers, but I still consider them to be rejects in their original form.

An example of the word "discography" being applied in relatively recent times to a catalog, or a listing of records by a certain artist, can be found in Louis P. Lochner's book *Fritz Kreisler* (London: Rockliff, 1950). It simply lists the titles of Fritz Kreisler's records numerically, from 1910 to 1950, with no allusion to location, date (however vague), matrix number, or take, disregarding the rare and valuable sides the great violinist made in Berlin prior to 1910. Whereas in earlier times we had a discography, albeit a perfunctory one, described as a listing, here we have a listing bearing the dignity of the term "discography."

Next we come to consider in detail the various jazz and dance band discographies. As the latest of these are my own, I will simply say that they follow the format outlined in the last paragraph but one, with the personnel of each band, or what I believe after intense study of the subject to be the personnel, surmounting each session. The various editions of *Hot Discography* by Charles Delaunay were, as we have seen, true pioneers in their field of research. All four completed books present their contents neither alphabetically by artist (the most obviously suitable manner, as jazz collectors are concerned primarily with the artist) nor by title (impracticable, in view of the enormous repetition of titles in jazz recordings, apart from which the title is of less importance in jazz than in any other form of music; what matters here is the treatment of the title by the *artist*). Instead, a kind of rough and very arbitrary chronology is used, which varies somewhat from edition to edition. This is maintained for the earlier recordings considered by the author to be of sufficient importance. Other subsequent and presumably less valuable recordings are given an alphabetical listing in the second half. For the most part, matrix numbers are used, takes never are, locations are conspicuous in their absence, and dates are roughly lumped together in the manner of Bauer. In *New Hot Discography*, greater attention is given to dates, but the continued use of chronology according to style of music makes reference very difficult. The uncompleted serialized form attempted by Delaunay introduced biographical notes, and at last an acceptable alphabetical presentation.

Orin Blackstone's offset typescript *Index to Jazz* presents the records alphabetically according to artist, with some cross-references where pseudonyms were used, but lists each record by catalog number, not matrix number, with a rather rough format for personnels. Matrix numbers and takes are sometimes shown, and important artists are given bold headings and a cross-reference to records they made under names other than their own. The neat dimensions of the four volumes, and the easy-reference format of the presentation of the information, make them ideal *vade mecum* for forays into junk shops, large collections being sold piece-meal, and anywhere jazz collectors' items can be found.

Jazz Directory, the promising but ill-fated British essay in jazz discography, also appeared in a readily referable form. The sessions are sorted out according to chronology, the artists alphabetically, many matrix numbers and some takes are shown, and many catalog numbers more than either of its predecessors, are divulged. Printed in light and heavy plantain, on good quality paper, this was, during its lifetime, the standard jazz discography that eclipsed the others. It included all known blues records, and as many recorded examples as could be traced of black preachers and their congregations, yet studiously omitted a wide variety of dance band records that had at least as much right to inclusion in a book with the word "jazz" in its title. The inherent weakness in a discography of this kind, be it Delaunay's, Blackstone's, or McCarthy's, is that they all attempted to include the latest jazz records, actual or alleged, along with the earlier recordings, with the result that in an effort to be up-to-date, none of them ever was. The survivors of the jazz era of the 1920s and 1930s continued to make records, and those who followed in their footsteps, or blazed new trails of their own in the name of "progressive" jazz or some other guise, added to the problem. Bauer pointed the way by establishing a cut-off date for *Historical Records* (even if failing to note that they were all vocal and mostly operatic) at 1908-1909. Critics may quibble at his choice of a date for the end of his survey, but by including it in the title of his book, clearly marked on the spine, he led no one into thinking that records of Titta Ruffo, Fedor Chaliapin, or Ernestine Schumann-Heink made after 1908 would be listed, or that records by Tito Schipa, Toti dal Monte, or Amelita Galli-Curci would be included at all.

For this reason, when I set out in 1952 to produce a definitive jazz discography as the first of a series of major works of this kind, I determined to follow Bauer's example and employ a date at which to conclude the research. The first edition was a loose-leaf affair that made the mistake of including blues records, but when this very limited edition was exhausted, and the demand continued, it was soon apparent that the market for a blues discography was somewhat different from that for a survey on jazz records. Accordingly, all subsequent editions have only included blues records if the singer is accompanied by a jazz band or one or two obvious jazz artists. I was pleased to make the acquaintance of two of the world's principal authorities on blues and gospel music, W. J. Godrich and Robert M. W. Dixon, who have enterprisingly produced two beautiful editions of *Blues and Gospel Records, 1902-1942*, again using date boundaries. As we have seen, a third edition is at this writing almost complete. The format follows that of *Jazz Records, 1897-1942*, with the added detail of the exact day of the week on which a session took place. Meticulous research can ask no more than that.

The date 1942 was chosen as the most suitable one at which to end both the jazz and the blues discographies as it was on July 31 of that year that the American Federation of Musicians instructed its members to withhold their services from recording (see chapter 1). By the time recording was generally resumed late in 1944, the jazz scene was still undergoing a cataclysmic change, and to some extent the blues field was showing signs of alteration. Bauer had his reasons for concluding his work at 1908-1909; he does not give them in his foreword to *Historical Records*, but alludes to a subsequent volume covering 1909 to 1925, and a third to include artists who recorded on cylinders and other vertical-cut records. These volumes do not seem to have materialized.

Given the foundation provided by Delaunay, Blackstone, McCarthy, and (I like to think) myself, to some extent, other discographers have set out to investigate in greater depth the known or supposed recordings of individual jazz soloists. Thus, we have the works of Walter C. Allen already referred to (*King Joe Oliver* and *Hendersonia*), Howard J. Waters' *Jack Teagarden's Music*, also published by Walter C. Allen, and a remarkable book on *Clarence Williams* (Tom Lord, Chigwell, Essex, England: Storyville, 1976), all of which investigate with exactness and thoroughness the many hundreds of records these artists have made. Similar volumes have appeared on such subjects as Duke Ellington, Bix Beiderbecke, and Louis Armstrong, but apart from the discography on Bix Beiderbecke in Richard M. Sudhalter's biography *Bix: Man and Legend* (New York: Arlington House, 1974, with Philip R. Evans), which offers the same minute attention to detail, these follow a rather more rough-hewn path.

There is a good discography in the form of an appendix to Charles Delaunay's biography of Django Reinhardt, the gypsy guitarist who has become the best-known jazz soloist not of American citizenship. It is quite the most outstanding discographical work ever produced by Delaunay, for it gives as much known detail as the above-mentioned American works.

Although my own *Jazz Records* extends the frontiers back to 1897 and so includes a fairly large selection of pre-jazz ragtime recordings, only one book has so far been devoted to ragtime exclusively. This is *Recorded Ragtime, 1897-1958* (David Jasen, Hamden, Conn.: Shoe String Press, 1973). It is one of the very few works of its kind to be produced by a practicing musician, and though it includes no matrix or take numbers, no exact recording dates (details of these are given to a month only), and lists the items in two alphabetical sections under title and composer, it is an absolute *sine qua non* for ragtime and its kindred forms. The purist may object to the inclusion of certain titles and certain artists and/or composers, but as an all-embracing reference book on the subject, it is beyond reproach.

Mention must also be made of two other important discographies, both published by Arlington House, New York. One is by D. Russell Connor and Warren W. Hicks, published in 1969 under the title *B.G. on the Record.* It details all the known recordings of all kinds, jazz and serious alike, by Benny Goodman, clarinetist. There are indices showing titles, films, other artists, and so on, and through the discographical body of the book there runs an informative and entertaining narrative amounting to a biography of Benny Goodman. The other is *Moonlight Serenade,* subtitled *A Bio-Discography of the Glenn Miller Civilian Band* (John Flower, 1972), which follows a pattern similar to the Connor-Hicks's book. It should be pointed out that in these two volumes, details of radio transcription records are given.

It is but a short step from the world of jazz to that of dance music, and of course any book on the latter is bound to duplicate at least some of the contents of the former—as I discovered when I compiled *British Dance Bands, 1912-1939* (with Edward Walker, Chigwell, Essex, England: Storyville, 1973) and *The American Dance Band Discography, 1917-1942* (New York: Arlington House, 1975). These follow exactly the same format as my other discographies. It is encouraging to note that Horst Lange's fine German discography (see chapter 2) is cast in a very similar mold. If there is a weakness in this format, it lies in the absence of an index to individual musicians' names. The same weakness is apparent in my *British Dance Bands,* but this will be corrected in future editions.

In presenting my *Discography of Historical Records on Cylinders and 78s* (Westport, Conn.: Greenwood Press, 1978), I adopted the same outline as all the other books I have compiled that claim to be discographies without using the word in the titles. I added biographical details in note form to each chapter on the individual speakers (I did the same in *The Complete Entertainment Discography*). There are no indices to either book, as the main part of each is its own index. Thus, a collector, researcher, or other historian wishing to find details of the career of a politician, sportsman, popular singer, or comedian known or suspected to have made records simply turns to the appropriate section in the body of the book.

In the 1960s and after, a new form of discography has made its appearance: the label listing. It may be appropriate to term this "pure" discography, since its primary concern is with the recording of *all* kinds of music and sound, not with the music and sound themselves. I have already referred to the sterling work of Carl Kendziora in researching the Plaza-American Record Corporation-CBS series, and the Perfect dance records booklet, and to the joint work of Bill Bryant and Tim Brooks on pre-1911 American Columbias. There are also, it should be noted, a number of booklets available, compiled by English researcher Jim Hayes, on the Edison Bell eight-inch Radio label, the nine-inch Crown, the first thousand English Brunswicks (1930-1934), the English Decca "popular" ten-inch issues of 1929-1934, and the Decca-promoted Edison Bell Winners of 1933-1935. These, however, make no claim to be discographies. They are numerical catalogs without "in-depth" discographical details, but for anyone researching any kind of music likely to have been issued on any of these labels within the stated limits, the booklets are essential tools.

In 1969, I published my first label listing myself. Believing it to be of such limited appeal that no publisher would consider it, I soon discovered that I was quite wrong, and I make no secret of the fact that with considerable help from my colleague and friend Walter C. Allen, and, since his death, from his widow Ann Allen, some 1,500 copies were sold. In view of the fact that the subject matter was the recordings made for and usually issued on the domestic black-labeled Victor, and the subsidiary Bluebird, Electradisk, Timely Tunes, and Sunrise labels from the beginning of electric recording in 1925 to the end of the block of matrix numbers then in use in 1936, this demonstrated the keen interest among all kinds of collectors in detailed accounts of all kinds of recorded sound. I have since been asked countless times for a *complete* Victor discography, at least of 78s, and it is quite possible that such an encyclopedic work will be forthcoming.

Brief reference was made in chapter 2 to Allen Koenigsberg's work on Edison cylinders and to Raymond R. Wile's volume on Edison disc records. Both are exhaustive accounts of the repertoire of the earliest cylinders and the Edison Diamond Discs. The cylinders are listed according to artist and title, with a cross-reference to the date of issue of each (there are no dates of recording shown except for the exact transcriptions from Edison's *First Book of Phonograph Records,* from May 24, 1889, to April 23, 1892), and the result is a large, easily referable, complete account of exactly what the North American Phonograph Company did record for its showmen-customers. A more valuable historical document of its kind could hardly be imagined or desired.

The book devoted to Edison Diamond Discs shows the latter-day lateral-cut Edison records also; details of everything concerning thousands of issues between 1912 and 1929 are shown in clear type: catalog number, matrix number, date of issue, title, composer, artist credit, deletion date; all are noted painstakingly, with one important omission—the recording date. As the original recording ledgers or files still exist, it seems a great pity that this most important piece of information was not included. This is the only weakness in the work. Otherwise it must take a place in the library of any seat of learning or individual research worker.

Something similar, though less detailed generally, has been the preoccupation over some thirty years of J. R. Bennett, who from 1955 has provided us with small booklets published by Oakwood Press in England. These have covered numerical listings of all vocal records issued in the "His Master's Voice" catalogs of Britain, France, Germany, and Italy, including the popular items as well as the more serious and operatic issues, but with few recording dates and only rather sketchy matrix number details. Dates of issue are usually shown and, where known, the composers; there is also an artist index. In the same series, known as *Voices of the Past,* J. R. Bennett is also represented by a volume on Dischi Fonotipia, the Italian pioneer label that preserved with magnificent recording technique the voices of so many of the greatest opera singers of the turn of the century, and he assisted Eric Hughes with a volume on the "His Master's Voice" International "Red Label" Catalog. Michael Smith contributed a companion work on the same make's Black Label Catalogue and on Columbia vocal issues. Despite the omissions of recording dates and, of course, all rejected sides, these books are also of incalculable importance to the student of records generally and recorded vocal art in particular.

Because almost every label, from the most expensive "celebrity" category to the humblest popular kind sold in chain stores for a few cents each, contains a percentage of material of some interest culturally or historically, often both, it seems that a series of books devoted to these labels is very much needed. Using sources I outlined in chapter 3 and presenting them along the lines I have suggested above, it should be within the bounds of possibility that over the coming years most if not all the 78 rpm records ever made (at least in the United States and Europe) could be detailed in a correctly presented, accurately compiled series of volumes. A start has been made; may it continue and prosper.

5

Securing Information about Discographies

THERE WAS a time, not very long ago, when the appearance of a full-length discography would warrant no attention from the press, either in the United States or Great Britain. The specialist magazines, run on a shoestring budget, would obviously review whatever came within their particular scope, and Britain's *Gramophone* would comment on any book concerning records of any kind, from whatever angle.

Now, in the late 1970s, it is a very different matter. I can speak without boasting, I hope, of my own experiences at the hands of the press following the appearance of my *Complete Entertainment Discography, Jazz Records, 1897-1942*, and *The American Dance Band Discography, 1917-1942*. They received reviews, often of gratifying length, in such widely different periodicals as the monthly *Hobbies, The New Yorker, Stereo Review* (all New York), the *Sunday Plain Dealer* (Cleveland), the *Washington International Arts Letter*, the *Sanford Herald* (North Carolina), and the *Santa Barbara News Press* (California).

Obviously, a discography of entertainment personalities will not be of great interest to a jazz enthusiast, nor will a jazz discography appeal strongly to a collector of opera or cinema organ records, and the many magazines throughout the world designed for jazz aficionados would be the obvious source of information about the format, style, and contents of *Jazz Records* (and possibly *The American* [or *British*] *Dance Bands*). Similarly, England's *The Record Collector* would carry a review of any discography concerned with all great vocalists, or perhaps with only one.

The following is a listing of the actual publications which are known to review discographies, most of them on a general basis, some as specialist magazines:

American Library Association (New York)

American Reference Books Annual (Littleton, Colo.)

The Antique Phonograph Monthly (Brooklyn, N.Y.)

The Arts (San Francisco)

Billboard (Los Angeles, mainly concerned with theatrical discographies)

Book Review Monthly (New York)

Books and Bookmen (London)

The Boston Ledger

The Box Office (New York)

Buena Park News (California)

Cashbox (New York)

Choice (Middletown, Conn.)

Coda (Toronto, Canada, designed principally for jazz and blues collectors)

Down Beat (New York, aimed at the professional musician, but enjoys a circulation among jazz and blues enthusiasts)

Good Times (Lowell, Mass.)

Gramophone (London)

The Gunn Report (Essex, Eng.; a magazine for 78 rpm collectors of all kinds, principally of the more popular forms of music)

Hi-Fi News and Record Review (London; a technical paper that nevertheless does review discographies of all kinds)

Hobbies (New York)

Host (New York)

Hyde Park Tribune (Massachusetts)

Jazz Journal International (London)

Knickerbocker News (New York)

Library Journal (New York)

Lincoln University (Pennsylvania)

Matrix (London; a duplicated paper, almost exclusively concerned with individual-artist discographies itself)

Melody Maker (London; the "Bible" of British popular-music musicians for over half a century, now concerned mainly with "pop" music, but still spares space for a discography of any aspect of this and its forerunners)

Mississippi Rag

Music Journal (New York)

Music Library Association (New York)

Musical Theater (New York)

Nashville Banner (Tennessee)

New West (Beverly Hills, Calif.)

The New Yorker

Philadelphia Daily News

The Record Collector (Ipswich, Eng.; concerned only with classical vocal records)

Record Research (Brooklyn, N.Y.; primarily concerned with jazz, blues, and ragtime in all their forms, but often carries articles and discographies of

bygone popular artists, dance and light orchestras, even occasionally concert
  singers and pianists)
Recorded Sound (London; the official organ of the British Institute of Recorded
  Sound, in which have been published in nearly thirty years discographies
  of singers, pianists, violinists, music hall artists, American and British bands,
  and theatrical personalities)
Records and Recording (London; technical publication carrying reviews of impor-
  tant books on records, including discographies)
San Diego Union
Sanford Herald (North Carolina)
Santa Barbara News Press
The Second Line (New Orleans; devoted to the study of original jazz)
Sounds Vintage (London; designed for collectors of old records, phonographs
  and other machines, radio sets, piano rolls and players, etc.)
Stereo Review (New York)
Storyville (Essex, Eng.; concerned with classic jazz in all forms, blues and gospel,
  ragtime, certain kinds of dance music; the study of these and presentation of
  facts concerning them, profusely illustrated with unusual photographs)
Sunday Plain Dealer (Cleveland, Ohio)
Talking Machine Review (Bournemouth, Dorset, Eng.; similar policy to *Sounds
  Vintage,* but not concerned with anything other than records and machines;
  catalogs reprinted, LPs and relevant books reviewed)
Variety (New York; the long-established news magazine of the entertainment
  profession generally)
Washington International Arts Letter
Wilson Library Bulletin (New York)
Wisconsin Newspaper Association

There are probably other sources of information in various areas of
the press all over the world. (For example, the Milan-based magazine
Musica sometimes carries notification on a new discography, and the
French jazz collectors' periodical *Le Jazz Hot,* founded in the 1930s by
Charles Delaunay and the late Hugues Panassié, of course advises its
readers of the coming of discographies likely to interest them.)

I am sometimes asked if I have any plans for producing any sort of
discographical work on records made since my usual "cut-off" date of
1942, or at least continuing from there until the end of 78s in the very late
1950s, or even covering long-playing records. My answer generally is
"No." The period itself, and the music it produced, does not interest
me personally, and I prefer to leave its study and documentation to those
for whom it has some appeal: each one to his taste. There is so much
more research to be done on records made prior to 1942—because so
relatively little was committed to print at the time compared with the
contemporary documentation since—that I feel I can serve the interests

of students of recorded sound better by concentrating on the aspect that interests me most. One day there will have to be a comprehensive discography of "pop" music, with full details of the changes in personnel of the various groups, the dates of recording, and so on, and if "pop" as the word is currently understood still holds its meaning and power then, no doubt the media will stampede into reviewing such a discography. As intimated at the beginning of this chapter, the appearance of a booklength discography now is more worthy of media acknowledgment than it was ten or twenty years ago. The burgeoning of nostalgia as a marketable commodity has meant the wholesale reissue of old 78 rpm recordings of many kinds. This in turn means that more people are seeking more details of what similar recordings may have been made and issued, and the various magazines and other publications are doing excellent work in keeping all sections of the public informed.

TESSARI, Gino. (Baritone). (Debut: Zara 1890)

Black G. & T., Milano, 1903.

52629	Favorita: Vien Leonora	Donizetti

1904.

52447	Germania: L'eroico del I atto	Franchetti
52456	Faust: Dio possente	Gounod

TETRAZZINI, Elvira. (Soprano). (1867-...)

Black & Silver Columbia, Milano, 1904.

10298	Manon Lescaut: In quelle trine morbide (7")	Puccini
10295	Zazà: Non so capir perchè (w. Baldassare) (7")	Leoncavallo
10296	Don Giovanni: Là ci darem la mano (w. Baldassare)	Mozart
10328	Educande di Sorrento: Un bacio rendimi (w. Baldassare)	Usiglio

July 1904.

10392	Traviata: Un dì felice (w. Santini)	Verdi
10393	Lucia di Lammermoor: Verranno a te (w. Santini)	Donizetti
10394	Rigoletto: È il sol dell'anima (w. Santini)	Verdi
10395	Amico Fritz: Quei fiori son per me (w. Santini)	Mascagni
10396	Amico Fritz: Tutto tace (w. Santini) (7")	Mascagni
10397	Adriana Lecouvreur: Tu sei la mia corona (w. Santini) (7")	Cilea

Fonodisc, Milano, 1906-07.

141	Traviata: Addio del passato	Verdi
148	Il libro santo	Pinsuti
250	Nuvole bianche	Roessinger
251	Ave Maria	Cherubini
307	Bohème: Mi chiamano Mimì	Puccini
465	Forza del destino: La vergine degli angeli	Verdi
97	Don Giovanni: Là ci darem la mano (w. Baldassare)	Mozart
133	Bohème: Dite ben (w. Baldassare)	Puccini
165	Rigoletto: Quartetto (w. Del Lungo, Acerbi & Baldassare) 1st part	Verdi
166	Rigoletto: Quartetto (w. Del Lungo, Acerbi & Baldassare) 2nd part	Verdi
189	Rigoletto: V'ho ingannato (w. Baldassare)	Verdi
298	Lucia di Lammermoor: Sestetto (w. Braglia, Zuffo & Galli)	Donizetti
305	Don Pasquale: Tornami dir che m'ami (w. Acerbi)	Donizetti
357	Rigoletto: Giovanna ho dei rimorsi (w. Acerbi)	Verdi
358	Rigoletto: È il sol dell'anima (w. Acerbi)	Verdi
373	Traviata: Un dì felice (w. Acerbi)	Verdi
462	Ernani: O sommo Carlo (w. Martinez-Patti & Baldassare)	Verdi
475	Traviata: Brindisi (w. Martinez-Patti)	Verdi

TETRAZZINI, Luisa. (Soprano) (a). (1871 Firenze-1940 Milano)
(Debut: Firenze 1890)

Dark Green Zonophone, U.S.A., 1904-05.

10000	Lucia di Lammermoor: Rondò (10 3/4")	Donizetti
10001	Rigoletto: Caro nome (10 3/4")	Verdi

Nänie, Op. 67 Orch.
§ Berlin Phil.—Cooper   Pol. 65905*

Polka, D major Strings*
Beethoven Qtt. (2ss)   USSR. 16228/9

Polonaise, Op. 55 Orch.
Moscow Radio—Golovanov   USSR. 015499
(Moussorgsky : Scherzo)

PRELUDES
B flat, Op. 46, No. 1
§ M. Rosenthal   P.E 11145 ; AmD. 25317

B minor, Op. 11
J. Flier   USSR. 14172
{Rubinstein : Polka)
▲ V. Sofronitzky   USSR. 17063

Unspecified
S. Peschko   D.K 28180
(below ;   & Cui : Impromptu-Caprice)
▲ M. Shapiro   JpC. 28895

(8) Russian Folk Dances, Op. 58 (or : Folk songs)
Orch.
Youth Sym.—Kondrashin   USSR. 17274/8
(5ss—Tchaikovsky : Snow Maiden, excerpt)
E.I.A.R. Sym.—Gui   P.BB 25074/5
(3ss—Scriabin : Rêverie)   o.n. CB 20238,9
▲ Sym. Orch.—Gobermann (YPR. n.d.)
§ Philadelphia—Stokowski (G.DB 2443 & DA 1415 ;
          Vic. 8491 & 1681)
L.S.O.—Coates   (G.D 1811.2 ;   AW 168/9 ;
          Vic. 9797/8)
Pasdeloup—Inghelbrecht Pat.X 5521/2)

... No. 4, Gnat's Dance
▲ Decca Sym. (D. Y5685 ; AmD. 23103)

... No. 6, Berceuse
Philharmonia—Dobrowen   G.C 3754
(Tchaikovsky : Serenade, s.7)   SL 109

Valse (unspec.)
S. Peschko   D.K 28180
(above; & Cui : Impromptu-Caprice)

**MISCELLANEOUS : Harmonisation of Russian
Liturgical Music—Chant of the last judgment**
I. Denissov (Bs), A. Labinsky (pf.)   BaM. 8
(Arrs. by Liapounov & Balakirev)

FOLK SONG ARRS. :
By the Brook ; Vanya ; The little town ; Lullaby
School Cho.   G.C 3527
(Warlock & Bridge)

... Lullaby only
§ J. Rogatchewsky (T) (C.D 6280)

ORCHESTRATION—See **Moussorgsky:** Sorochintsy Fair

LIAPOUNOV, Sergius Mikhailovich
          (1859-1924)
Berceuse, F sharp major, Op. 11, No. 1 pf.
L. Kentner   C.DX 932
(Walton : Façade, Valse)

Lezghinka, Op. 11, No. 10 (Caucasian Dance)
pf.
A. Brailowsky (2ss)   Vic. 11-8567

(The) Mountain pasture Male Cho.
Cho.—Ledkovsky   Pol. 11883
(Glinka : Partsong)

SONGS
Morning ; Oriental Ballad (or : Eastern Romance)
V. Viktorova (S)   USSR. 10044
(½s each—Balakirev : The Dream)

**MISCELLANEOUS : Harmonisation of Russian
Liturgical Music—Chant of Penitence**
I. Denissov (Bs), A. Labinsky (pf.)   BaM. 8
(Arrs. by Liadov & Balakirev)

LIEBESKIND, Joseph (1866-1916)

Symphony, No. 1, A minor
Swiss Radio Orch.—Haug (10ss) G.FKX 501/5

LISZT, Franz (1811-1886)

CLASSIFICATION (Based on that by H. Searle
          in " Grove ")

A. INSTRUMENTAL

I. Orchestra	(1) Original	(2) Arrangements
II. Pf. & Orch.	(1) Original	(2) Arrangements
III. Pf. solo	(1) Studies	(2) Various Original
	(3) Dance forms	(4) On National
		Themes
	(5) Paraphrases,	Operatic Transcrip-
	tions, etc.	
	(6) Partitions de Piano	

IV. Pf. 4 hands (Recordings only in Supplement)
V.   2 pfs.
VI. Organ
VII. Other Instruments (No recordings)

B. VOCAL
VIII. Opera (No recordings)
IX.   Sacred Choral Works
X.   Secular Choral Works (No recordings)
XI.   Songs with pf.
XII-XV. (No recordings)

C. MISCELLANEOUS

D. INDEX

A. INSTRUMENTAL
I. ORCHESTRAL (1) *ORIGINAL*

(A) Faust Symphony G.14 (with T & Cho.)
§ G. Jouatte, Vlassoff Cho. & Paris
Phil.—Meyrowitz (14ss)   C.LX 455 61
*(Pat PDT 31 7 ; C GQX 10804 10 ; AmC. 68747/53,
          set M 272 ; CanC. 15446 52, set D 79)*

Hungarian Storm March G.25
¶ L.S.O.—Coates   (G.DB 1647 ; Vic. 11471
          in set M 169)

Mazeppa[1]   G.6   (Sym. Poem No. 6)
Dresden Phil.—v. Kempen[2]   Pol. 68121 2
(3ss—Dvořák Slavonic Dance No. 2)
§ Berlin Phil.—Fried D.CA 8177 8 ; Pol. 66787 8
Sym. Orch — Knappertsbusch   P R 1579 81 ;
          Od.O-1189° 9 ; AmD. 20082 4

Mephisto Waltz[2] G.16 (2)
New York Phil. Sym.—Rodzinski
          AmC. 12580 1D
*(3ss—Wolf-Ferrari : Segreto, Overture)   set X 281
          (& LP : ML 2057)*

Florence May Festival—Markevitch
          P.BB 25158 9
(3ss—Mozart German Dance, K 605, No. 3)
          (Tem. (LP) TT 2038)

---

* From "Les Vendredis": See Glazounov.   [1] For pf see Sec III (1)
[2] The auto couplings (69174/5 in DGS set 14) appear to have on the 4th side. Un sospiro, played by Karolyi.
* No. 2 of 2 Episodes after Lenau's "Faust," for pf see Sec III (6), see also No. 3, Sec. III (3)

Sample page from Francis F. Clough and C. J. Cuming, *The World's
Encyclopaedia of Recorded Music* (Westport, Conn.: Greenwood Press,
1970).

Footlights Parade. DB1303.
I Want a Fair and Square Man.
   DB1309.
Not Bad. DB1368.
Nymph Errant. DB1297.
There's a Ring Around the Moon.
   DB1297.
Two Friends in Harmony. DB1333.
Way to Love. DB1303.
What a Pleasant Surprise. DB1314.
What Now? DB1368.
Who Do You Think You Are?
   DB1314.
You've Got Everything. DB1263.

COLUMBIA. Carroll Gibbons' Boy Friends,
   with Matt Malneck on violin.
On the Air. DB1001.
Till To-morrow. DB1001.

Gene Gifford's Orchestra.—H. Gene
Gifford, American guitarist, composer
and arranger, came into prominence
with the Casa Loma Orchestra.
For nearly five years he was an
active member of the Casa Loma, and
during that time was responsible for
many of the arrangements. His compositions during this time included
" Rhythm Man," " Smoke Rings,"
" Maniacs' Ball," " Blue Jazz,"
" White Jazz," and others.
In 1935 Gifford organised his own
recording combination in New York.
The unit recorded his four most recent
compositions.

1935.
GENE GIFFORD.   Arranger.
MATT MATLOCK.   Alto sax and
                        clarinet.
BUD FREEMAN.   Tenor sax.
BUNNY BERIGAN.   Trumpet.
MOREY SAMUEL.   Trombone.
CLAUDE THORNHILL.   Piano.
DICK MCDONOUGH.   Guitar.
PETE PETERSON.   Bass.
RAY BEAUDUC.   Drums.
WINGY MANNONE.   Vocals.

H.M.V. 1935.
Dizzy Glide. B8383.
New Orleans Twist. B8390.
Nothin' But the Blues. B8383.
Squareface. B8374.

The Gilt-Edged Four.—Between 1925
and 1927, a number of records were
issued by Columbia and credited to
the Gilt-Edged Four, a British combination used for recording purposes
only. The group also accompanied
certain vocal records by Ed. Lowry,
Ramon Newton and Buddy Lee.

COLLECTIVE ONLY.
AL STARITA.   Saxes, clarinet and
                        vocals.
VAN PHILLIPS.   Saxes.
MAX GOLDBERG.   Trumpet.
SID BRIGHT.   Piano.
LEN FILLIS.   Guitar.
MAX BACON.   Drums.
RUDY STARITA.   Drums and xylo-
                        phone.

COLUMBIA. 1925–1927.
Best Black. 3704.
Brotherly Love. 4311.
Cornfed. 4611.
Don't Bring Lulu. 3703.
Gonna Getta Girl. 4611.
Honey Bunch. 4002.
Hot Miss Molly. 3703.
I Can't Realise. 3710.
My Sugar. 3704.
Piccadilly Strut. 3840.
Tell All the World. 3711.
Tentin' Down in Tennessee. 4002.
Yiddisher Charleston. 4311.

Jean Goldkette.—Jean Goldkette,
American orchestra leader and pianist,
was born in France. Shortly after his
family moved to Russia, where Jean
received his education and musical
training.
In 1910 he went to America, and
later became the pianist with a small
concert combination at Lamb's Café
in Chicago. Then he moved to
Detroit, and in 1921 formed his first
dance orchestra. The combination
included Don Murray, saxes and clarinet; Joe Venuti, violin; Red Nichols,
trumpet; Paul van Loan and George
Crozier, trombones; Bill Kreutz, piano;
and Charles Harveth, drums. Three
years later the unit was re-organised.

1924–1928. COLLECTIVE.
JEAN GOLDKETTE.   Director.
FRANKIE TRUMBAUER.   Saxes and
                        clarinet.
DON MURRAY.   Saxes and
                        clarinet.
DOC RYKER.   Saxes and
                        clarinet.
DANNY POLO.   Saxes and
                        clarinet.
BIX BEIDERBECKE.   Trumpet.
RAY LUDWIG.   Trumpet.
FRED FARRAR.   Trumpet.
SPEIGAL WILCOX.   Trombone.
BILL RANK.   Trombone.
IZZY RISKIN.   Piano.
HOWDY QUICKSELL.   Banjo.
STEVE BROWN.   Bass.

Sample page from Hilton R. Schleman, *Rhythm on Record* (Westport, Conn.:
Greenwood Press, 1978).

RUTH BROWN:
Ruth Brown(vo)with

NYC,July 2,1952

869(3:17) Have a good time   Atl.973;Atco SD7009
870(2:53) Daddy daddy   -   EP535,LP8004,LP8080
                                  Atco SD7009

THE CLOVERS:
John "Buddy" Bailey(lead vo)Matthew McQuater(tenor vo)Harold Lucas
(baritone vo)Harold Winley(bass vo)Bill Harris(g)
                                  NYC,August 7,1952

871   One more kiss
872   Crawlin'   Atl.989,EP537,LP8009
873 (2:50)Yes,it's you   -   -   SD8162
874   Hey Miss Fannie   Atl.977,EP504   -
                                  Atco SD33-374

DIZZY GILLESPIE & HIS ORCHESTRA: (reissued from Blue Star)
Dizzy Gillespie(tp,vo)Don Byas(ts)Art Simmons(p)Joe Benjamin(b)
Bill Clark(dm)Humberto Morales(conga).
                                  Paris,March 25,1952

875   Cocktails for two(14776) Atl.EP521,LP142,LP1257
876   Moon nocturne   (14778)   Atl.   LP138
877   Cognac blues   (14777)   Atl.EP514,LP142,LP1257
878   Just one more chance(14781) -   -

WILBUR DE PARIS AND HIS RAMPART STREET PARADERS:
Sidney De Paris(tp,vo)Wilbur De Paris(tb)Omer Simeon(cl)Don
Kirkpatrick(p)Eddie Gibbs(bjo)Harold Jackson(b)Fred Moore(dm).
                                  NYC,September 11,1952

879   Hindustan   Atl.LP141,LP1208,LP1233
880   Shreveport stomp   Atl.LP143   -   -   EP511
881   The pearls   Atl.LP141   -
882   Tres moutarde   -   LP1208   -   EP511
883   When the Saints go marching in -   -   -   -
884   The Martinique   -   -
885   Under the double eagle Atl.LP143   -
886   Battle hymn of the Republic -   -
887   Prelude in C sharp minor Atl.LP141   -
888   Marchin' and swingin'   Atl.LP143   -
889   Sensation   -   LP1208

RAY CHARLES:
Ray Charles(p,vo)+tp,saxes,b,dm.

                                  NYC,September 11,1952

890   The sun's gonna shine again Atl.984,LP8025,LP8063,LP2-900
891 (2:34)Roll with me baby   Atl.976,LP8029
892   The midnight hour   -   LP8052
893 (2:43)Jumpin' in the morning Atl.984,LP8029

RUTH BROWN:
Ruth Brown(vo)with

                                  NYC,September 12,1952

894   Good for nothing Joe   Atl.978
895(3:58) Three letters   -   EP535;Atco SD7009
896   Love me or leave me

Sample page from Michel Ruppli, *Atlantic Records: A Discography* (Westport, Conn.: Greenwood Press, 1979).

54

JEF

? Jock Strachan and another-t/tb/2cl-ss-as/Asher Atkins-cl-ts/Leslie Jeffries-vn-ldr/Leon Zimbler-p/bj/bb/Bob
Tate-d/John Thorne-v.   London, late September, 1925.

C-7298-X	Just Like A Baby - vJT	Aco G-15816, Clm 1814, Sc 752
C-7299	Panama	Aco G-15814, Bel 856, Duo D-5090, Gmn 1804
C-7300	Babette (waltz)	Aco G-15816 - 895, Gmn 1807, Sc 750
C-7301	Collegiate	Aco G-15813, Bel 857, Clm 1817, Gmn 1803
	Desert Flower	- Sc 742
	The Hylton Medley	Aco G-15815, Gmn 1807
	If You've Got No Sweetie Of Your Own	Aco G-15817, Clm 1839
	Paradise	- Bel 879

London, October, 1925.

C-7372	I'm A Little Bit Fonder Of You	Aco G-15843, Duo B-5105, Gmn 1833
C-7373	The Baby Looks Like Me - vJT	Aco G-15841, Clm 1828, Mto S-1599
C-7374	Araby - vJT	Aco G-15842, Bel 879, Clm 1836, Duo B-5104,
		Gmn 1821, Mto S-1599, Sc 742
C-7375	? Savoy Christmas Medley	Aco G-15842, G-16083
C-7376	Charleston Mad	Aco G-15843, Bel 885, Clm 1834
C-7377	Poor Little Rich Girl	Aco G-15841 - -

London, November, 1925.

C-7460	Oh ! Boy, What A Girl - vJT	Aco G-15860, Bel 890, Clm 1852, Gmn 1835,
		Hom H-892
C-7461	Echoes Of Ireland	Aco G-15860, Bel 894, Gmn 1843
C-7462 ?	Bah-Bah-Bartholomew - vJT	Aco G-15861, Bel 891, Gmn 1835, Sc 751
C-7463	Tally Ho !	- Bel 894, Gmn 1837
C-7464	Paddlin' Madelin' Home - vJT	Aco G-15862, Bel 890, Clm 1847, Duo B-5124,
		Gmn 1837, Sc 756
C-7465 ?	Lovely Lady (waltz)	Aco G-15862, Bel 891

London, December, 1925.

C-7499	Ida - I Do	Aco G-15884, Clm 1852, Hom H-892
	Carolina Sweetheart (waltz)	- Sc 755
	I Love You - vJT	Aco G-15883
	Sunny Havana	- Bel 895, Clm 1847, Gmn 1848
	Comin' Home - vJT	Aco G-15885 -
	I Would Like To Know Why	- Sc 756

London, January, 1926.

C-7612	That's All There Is	Aco G-15908, Bel 923, Clm 1867, Gmn 1873
C-7616	The Tin Can Fusiliers - vJT	Aco G-15907 - Clm 1868, Gmn 1865
	Ukulele Baby - vJT	- Bel 924, Clm 1867 - Sc 757
	Keep Your Skirts Down, Mary Ann	Aco G-15908, Gmn 1875 -
	You Forgot To Remember (waltz)	Aco G-15909, Bel 924, Clm 1870
	The Bells Of St. Mary's	- Bel 925
	The Kinky Kids' Parade	Aco G-15910, Clm 1868
	Jalousie (tango)	Aco G-15913

London, February, 1926.

C-7705	My Castle In Spain - vJT	Aco G-15931, G-15996, Bel 943
C-7709	Along The Old Lake Trail	- Duo B-5152
	The Two Of Us - vJT	Aco G-15929, Bel 943, Clm 1871, Gmn 1884
	Who Loved You Best ?	
	April Blossoms - vJT	Aco G-15930, Duo B-5151
	Bambalina	- Bel 944 -

Bernard Miller-d replaces Tate.   London, March-April, 1926.

C-7759	Too Too	Aco G-15953, Clm 1885
C-7760	In Ukulele Avenue	Aco G-15952, Bel 965, Sc 764
C-7761	Matador - vJT	- Clm 1883, Gmn 1891, Sc 765
C-7763	Picador - vJT	Aco G-15953 - Duo B-5153 - -
	Oh, Lady, Be Good !	Aco G-15954, Duo B-5150
	Oh ! That Sweetie Of Mine	-
	Tres Jolie (tango)	Aco G-15960

Sample page from Brian Rust, *British Dance Bands, 1912-1939* (Chigwell, Essex, England: Storeyville Publications, 1973). Reprinted by permission.

This next date proves to be luckier than the last two, because the results were issued. It's the first of several versions of CANDY LIPS. No one seems certain about Ed Allen and Ed Cuffee. The clt/alt was listed as Arville Harris by Rust (10 - 1st ed.). In the 3rd edition he lists Ladnier, Harrison, Buster Bailey and Coleman Hawkins (all with Henderson in New York). He also lists Cyrus St. Clair, but there is no bbs present. In early research the names of Joe Smith (cnt), and Carmello Jejo (clt/alt) were also suggested for this session. This is Williams' only vocal version of CANDY LIPS. The verse words about... "Alice, in her pretty blue gown", give the reason for the interpolation in the January 25, 1927 version. The date is given by Rust and Godrich & Dixon (7) - possibly from Okeh files. The assignment of the adjacent matrix numbers is unknown.

EVA TAYLOR Contralto, Accomp. by Clarence Williams' Blue Seven
Eva Taylor (vcl), acc. possibly Ed Allen (cnt), possibly Ed Cuffee (tbn), unknown (clt/alt), possibly Arville Harris (ten), Clarence Williams (pno), probably Leroy Harris (bjo).   New York, Nov. 16, 1926

80214-A	CANDY LIPS (I'm Stuck on You)	Ok 8414-A, 40715-A
	(Jackson-Lauria)	
	(c. Mike Jackson-Jack Lauria; Mike Jackson & Jack Lauria, Aug. 23, 1926, CWMPC, Nov. 11, 1926)	

80215-A	SCATTER YOUR SMILES	Ok 8414-B, 40715-B
	(Kortlander-Wendling)	
	(c. Max Kortlander-Pete Wendling; Max Kortlander, Mar. 15, 1926; Shapiro, Bernstein, Apr. 23, 1926)	

The fact that this session was issued on both the 8000 series and the 40000 series, indicates the type of music played on this session. The arrangement of the introduction to CANDY LIPS was to be used in later sessions.

```
80214-A; Key of Ab                                    2:31
4 intro|16 verse|32 ch |32 ch                |32 ch
ens     |ET-ens  |ET-ens|16 reeds-ens/16 FA-ens|ET-ens

80215-A; Key of Eb                                    3:06
8 intro|16 verse|32 ch |32 ch          |32 ch |32 ch      |32 ch
ens     |ET-ens  |ET-ens|16 EA-ens/16 clt|ET-ens|12 EC/20 AH|ET-ens
```

                              *****

The remake session for Sadie Jackson (originally recorded October 29) took place on November 20th. The results were issued on Co 14181-D. Frank Driggs has stated that the pianist was Johnny Johnson. Perhaps he meant Jimmie Johnson, as it sounds like the latter to me. It does not sound like Clarence Williams, and is therefore listed with the Non-Clarence Williams recordings.

                              *****

A publicity release appeared in the November 10th New York AMSTERDAM NEWS announcing that the Ball of Silver Spring Lake Property Owners' Association would be held Friday, November 26th at the Renaissance Ballroom, 138th and 7th Ave., in New York. It would feature two orchestras, Lucille Hegamin, and the Clarence Williams Trio.

                              *****

Sample page from Tom Lord, *Clarence Williams* (Chigwell, Essex, England: Storeyville Publications, 1976). Reprinted by permission.

6

Labels

IT IS not entirely within the province of this book to delve deeply into the details of the countless labels under which some gems and an incalculable amount of rubbish have been issued over the years. Those of interest for one reason or another, of American origin, with British counterparts, have been covered by the present author in *The American Record Label Book* (New York: Arlington House, 1978), *from the Nineteenth Century Through 1942*, as the subtitle states. Nevertheless, it will doubtless be useful to readers to have some notes on the major labels, their life span, place of origin, variations in name, and any subsidiary labels produced by the same parent firm.

As we have seen at various points throughout earlier chapters, not all the works coming under the description of "discography" are concerned with an artist, a group of artists, or even a type of music. There have been several attempts at listing the known output of a certain make of record (in particular, the *Voices of the Past* booklets, compiled by John Bennett for Oakwood Press, and the duplicated but eminently serviceable booklets produced in Sweden by Kungliga Biblioteket on the various Swedish labels). I have already attempted a limited account of certain Victor recordings, and it is hoped that one day the entire accumulation of Victor repertoire from its beginning in 1900 will be published. In the press at the time of this writing I have a Berliner (British) discography, to be published by the Talking Machine Review in Bournemouth, Dorset, England, and a complete account of all English Decca 78s from 1929 to 1959, to be published by General Gramophone Publications Ltd. of Kenton, Middlesex. Similarly, there is no doubting the value of the Edison books by Allen Koenigsberg (cylinders) and Raymond Wile (discs).

It is hoped that the following notes will be of supplementary interest to the preceding chapters and perhaps be a starting point for research by a discographically-minded historian in years to come.

AJAX

This was a product of the Compo Company of Lachine, Quebec, Canda, under the management of H.S. Berliner, son of Emile, inventor of the gramophone disc record. The head office of Ajax ("The Quality Race Record") was in Chicago, however, although recording was mostly done in New York, somewhat less in Montreal.

The repertoire was mostly blues singing, some jazz (not necessarily all of it by black artists), and a little country-style music. Although the name was registered by Berliner in Canada on November 2, 1921, the earliest known Ajax records date from the summer of 1923. The label survived into the first months of electric recording, but disappeared in the spring of 1925. Evidently, at least some of the masters were sold to Pathé, since in January 1926 a few of them began to appear on that label and its subsidiary, Perfect.

Not all the titles appearing on Ajax were original recordings. Certain dance band and jazz records from the Plaza Music Company's catalog (Banner, Domino, Regal, and others) were also included in the Ajax releases, giving the lie to the advertising slogan about its being a quality *race* record. That it is a quality product is undeniable; acoustic or electric, the recording is usually excellent, the surfaces smooth. As might be expected, since the majority of the records issued in the eighteen months or so of the life of the label were by jazz or blues artists, they have been extensively covered by the various discographies on these subjects.

ANTHOLOGIE SONORE

A French label introduced in the 1930s, designed to perpetuate the music of preclassic times. Pressed by Pathé-Marconi in Paris, with striking gold labels printed in black, the repertoire is remarkably fine, superbly well-recorded on excellent laminated pressings. The war caused inevitable interruption of the program, but this was resumed soon after the end of hostilities until sometime in the 1950s. Much of the music, the works of fourteenth- to seventeenth-century composers, has seldom if ever been duplicated on other, better-known labels.

ARTO

The Arto Company of Orange, New Jersey, was a subsidiary of the Standard Music Roll Company of the same city, and from the late summer of 1920 to the autumn of 1922, the Arto label produced about two hundred issues of dance, jazz, and popular vocal items. The same, or very similar, repertoire also appeared simultaneously on such labels as Ansonia, Cleartone, Bell, and Globe. The last two continued to appear for some time after Arto had ceased, Bell lasting until 1928 (deriving its catalog from Emerson, then Gennett, both q.v.)

Arto products also occur on the West Coast label Nordskog, q.v., but as far as is known, nothing from its catalog was ever issued outside the United States. The recording studio was in New York, but there is evidence that more than one was used, and this may account for the fact that in the two years of its life, the Arto label used at least six different blocks of matrix numbers (one for each studio location?). It should be noted that the catalog numbers of Arto records are in step with those of Cleartone and Hy-Tone, except that the latter substitute the letters C or K for the figure 9 of Arto (most Arto records are numbered in a 9000 block), Bell, while in the Arto group, prefixed its numbers P, and Globe simply deducted two thousand numbers from that of whatever Arto issue was being duplicated by Globe.

AUTOGRAPH

Some six months before Victor and Columbia embarked on their course of recording electrically, Autograph had already adopted an electric recording system of its own. The labels of the records testify to this, although it must be said that the results do not bear comparison with the Western-Electric products of the two major firms. They are, however, noticeably more brilliant—if rather shrill—than the average acoustic recording of the time, and there are bass frequencies not enountered on the latter.

The majority of Autograph records have no catalog numbers, which suggests that they were made for private concerns (theaters, music stores, religious bodies, and so on) or individual artists or groups of artists, even perhaps at their own expense on occasion. The existence of an unnumbered record under the Rialto label, produced by (or for) the music house of that name at 330 South State Street, Chicago, but bearing a matrix number denoting obvious origin in the Marsh Recording Laboratories of 78 East Jackson Boulevard (whence came Autograph), tends to give credence to this suggestion. Among the Autograph records that do bear catalog numbers are several by the pioneer theater organist, Jesse Crawford. These were announced as being on sale in October 1924, at $1.50 each, exactly twice as much as Victor, Columbia, and the other *major* labels were asking for precisely the same material (popular music). Undoubtedly, this could account for the extreme rarity of these records; you either paid to have them made, or you paid heavily for the results of someone else's work.

Autograph masters were also used by Pathé, Paramount, Gennett, and (in England) Edison Bell. The latter are also theater organ recordings, made by Jesse Crawford's successor Milton Charles, at the organ of the Tivoli Theater, Chicago. They are also electric recordings and of commendable quality.

It is known that Orlando R. Marsh, president of the laboratories in which Autograph records were made, began his business in 1921 or 1922 at the latest. He seems to have abandoned the Autograph label in 1925, but Paramount records exist that prove the studios were active in the spring of 1926, though not later as far as is known.

BANNER—*see* PLAZA MUSIC COMPANY

BELL—*see* ARTO

BELTONA—*see* DECCA AND VOCALION

BERLINER

Emile Berliner, inventor of the flat disc containing sound recorded in a laterally-cut groove, was an immigrant to the United States from Hanover. He was born there in 1851, and made his home in Washington, D.C. in 1870. Before he was forty, he had put his scientific knowledge to use in producing the prototype of the records bearing his name, and in 1894 he launched his enterprise as a means of home entertainment. (Previous to this, most of his recordings, five-inch discs to be played on hand-driven phonographs and designed principally as toys, had been sold with the machines in Germany by Messrs. Kämmerer and Reinhardt, toy manufacturers and wholesalers.)

In 1895, Berliner was introduced to Eldridge R. Johnson, a mechanic in Camden, New Jersey, who produced a spring-driven machine to play the discs. After much legal wrangling with his agent, Frank Seaman, who tried to invade Berliner's territory with a blatant copy of both records and machine he called Zon-O-Phone (q.v.), Berliner joined forces with Johnson, and in 1901, the Victor Talking Machine Company was launched. Meanwhile, in the summer of 1898, Berliner's European emissary, Fred Gaisberg, had established headquarters of the branch in London, and was engaged in recording all kinds of music in a basement studio in Maiden Lane, behind the Strand. London proved a happy hunting ground for talent, but young Gaisberg and his colleague Sinkler Darby embarked on several European tours, recording extensive programs in countries as far apart as Russia and Spain. They returned to London after a further brief tour of Scotland, Ireland, and Wales, recording local talent, and in the summer of 1900 began recording on wax blocks, as devised in Camden by Eldridge Johnson. Hitherto, as shown in chapter 1, recording had been done on a zinc-etched disc; the new method, which was to remain materially unchanged for nearly half a century, promoted a smoother sound and more even surface for the finished pressing made from it.

Berliner's records had been five- and seven-inch since the beginning in 1894; gradually the five-inch were phased out, and in the summer of 1901, the very rare ten-inch Berliner record appeared. All the details of performance, including (as we have seen) the date of recording as a rule, were etched by hand or embossed on the smooth center area; labels were unknown. Johnson, before joining Berliner in the Victor project, had introduced seven-inch records with labels—"Improved Gram-O-Phone Records" he called them—in the summer of 1900 in the United States, but paper labels, making no reference to Berliner, did not appear in Europe until the autumn of 1901. It was not until 1924 that the Canadian Victor and Canadian HMV labels ceased to refer to the parent company as the Berliner Gram-O-Phone Company of Montreal, Ltd.

BLACK SWAN

This label was the product of the Pace Phonograph Corporation of New York. It was supposedly all-black, in its financing, its production, and its artists, but this in fact was only partly true. While original recordings for the label were commissioned by Harry Pace, black entrepreneur and one-time partner of black bandleader William C. Handy, and were performed by black artists, several masters were leased from other sources and issued on Black Swan although they were by white performers. Such sources as Paramount and Olympic were drawn on in this way, the real identities of the artists being disguised as a rule by the noncommittal name "Henderson's Dance Orchestra," "The Jazz Masters," and others.

Most Black Swan records are jazz collectors' or blues collectors' items, although both recording and surface qualities leave much to be desired. The first issue was in May 1921, and the last in July 1923. The following April, Paramount announced that ninety Black Swan records were available on its Race series, and indeed these contained the Black Swan trademark and the original catalog number on the Paramount label, in addition to the new Paramount number and the spread-eagle, the bird of a very different feather from the Black Swan that had preceded it.

BLUE NOTE

Probably the first label ever to cater exclusively to the jazz enthusiast, Blue Note flourished from 1939 until the 1960s, covering original recordings of prominent jazz musicians of all persuasions, and still very active into the long-playing era. The label did not depend on any other, and apart from some postwar issues on Vogue in Britain and France, no label has depended on it. There seem to have been several recording studios used to make Blue Note records, all in New York City, where the company headquarters was located.

BRUNSWICK

The first Brunswick records were issued in 1916, by a firm of piano manufacturers long established in Dubuque, Iowa, as the Brunswick-Balke-Collender Company. The headquarters of the recording division seems to have been in Chicago, but as the business expanded, studios were set up in New York and Los Angeles. The original issues were vertical-cut, but in January 1920, the first lateral-cuts were announced and proved very successful by virtue of their excellent technical quality and the roster of artists.

Throughout the 1920s, Brunswick was a flourishing concern, taking over the Vocalion Company in 1925, and establishing a European market in 1923. (In England, the music publishing house of Chappell was the "sole concessionaires," as the labels put it; in 1927, British Brunswick was formed under the management of Count Anthony de Bosdari, but this venture foundered in the autumn of 1929.) Soon after the Wall Street disaster of October 29, 1929, Brunswick sold out to Warner Brothers, the film company in Hollywood, but as the Depression grew, Warners themselves sold out to the newly formed American Record Corporation in December 1931. Brunswick then became the most expensive label in the combine (seventy-five cents, while the others sold at thirty-five cents each). Its career continued along with Vocalion, Banner, Melotone, Oriole, Perfect, and Romeo under the ARC aegis until the Columbia Broadcasting System reactivated the Columbia label, bought out ARC, and gradually phased Brunswick out altogether by April 1940.

In its somewhat turbulent quarter-century life, Brunswick firmly established overseas agencies in France, Germany, and Scandinavia. After the collapse of British Brunswick in September 1929, the label was not represented in Britain until Warner-Brunswick formed a new company and began marketing the records again in December 1930, using almost exactly the same label design as before. This continued until Decca assumed control of the label in June 1933 and maintained it for more than thirty years. It is worth noting that the surfaces of German Brunswick pressings prior to 1939 are truly superb, infinitely superior to those of any of their sister labels in other countries, the United States included.

The principal subsidiary, Melotone, was introduced in the autumn of 1930, during the Warner Brothers era, and the following spring, Britain followed with a label called Panachord that looked exactly like its American counterpart, except of course for the brand name (and even this was displayed in flowing copperplate style like Melotone's). Melotone lived as a thirty-five-cent label until April, 1938. Decca dispensed with Panachord in November 1939. Prior to these, in England there had been an alliance between British Brunswick and the Duophone Syndicate. On the latter's Duophone label, which looked not unlike Brunswick with its shield design, it was and sometimes still is possible to find examples of first-class American dance bands, cloaked by the most outlandish pseudonyms, recorded in New York for Duophone by the Brunswick-Balke-Collender Company, most of them never issued in America at all. Not all Duophone records relate to Brunswick, however; the first issues under this trademark in 1925 drew from Vocalion, certainly, but from sometime in 1927 to the autumn of 1928, Duophone had access to the Emerson repertoire, q.v. Those that were pressed from American Brunswick masters appeared as black-label unbreakable records made of thin plastic (carrying the grooves) pressed on a light but tough cardboard-type base, and as violet-label normal pressings. It need hardly be added that the latter, for all their fragility, are indisputably the superior product.

CAMEO

The Cameo Record Corporation of New York began issuing records in February 1922. They were originally sold by Macy's stores at fifty cents each, but later, during the phonograph boom years, they widened their business horizons and even produced sister labels (they were not subsidiaries, as they carried the same price tags and the same repertoire, albeit frequently under other names than those used by Cameo itself.) These labels—Lincoln, Muse, Romeo, and Tremont—were apparently zoned into different areas of the United States. The only one to last was Romeo; it became one of the strings to the American Record Corporation's bow in 1931, and was maintained by ARC until April 1938.

Cameo joined forces with the Pathé Phonograph and Radio Corporation early in 1928, and from that point until the combine became part of the ARC empire and Cameo was discontinued, it is possible to find Perfect and Cameo interchanging material and co-issuing it sometimes under a pseudonym, sometimes using the same name on both.

CAPITOL

Capitol Records, Inc., was founded in 1942 in Los Angeles by the composer and singer Johnny Mercer. It has become one of the major American labels of the last four decades, and although unrepresented in Britain until December 1948, first as a Decca associate and since January 1956 as one of the strongest links in the EMI chain, it very quickly became recognized as an important label in the popular field, and has also contributed a fair share of fine classic records on LP.

CETRA

This is an Italian label concerned entirely with serious music, starting its career in Turin in 1937 and continuing into the 1970s. The name is the Italian word for a zither, and the trademark is a stylized representation of this instrument. The letters of the word are the initials of the parent company: Compagnia Edizioni Teatro Registrazioni ed Affini. For a time, examples from the Cetra catalog were issued in England on the Parlophone Odeon and HMV labels.

CHAMPION—see GENNETT

CLARION—see COLUMBIA

CLIMAX—see COLUMBIA

COLUMBIA

Whole books could be written about the story and ramifications of the Columbia label, from its earliest days as the only prospering subsidiary—the Columbia Phonograph Company of Maryland, Delaware, and the District of Columbia—of the North American Phonograph Company, through its transference to the British branch of what was then known as the Columbia Graphophone Company, its almost total extinction after the heavy blows of the Wall Street collapse in 1929, and its resurgence nine or ten years later, when William S. Paley, president of the Columbia Broadcasting System, bought the American Record Corporation (of which Columbia had become a dormant affiliate) and reactivated the label in September 1939, to resume its place of vigorous leadership in the American record market.

This is not the book in which such a story can be told. I have attempted to cover as much of it as can be told in a single chapter in my book *The American Record Label Book* (New York: Arlington House, 1978), but the definitive account remains to be written. Suffice it for this present work to say that although Columbia's earliest recordings were in cylinder form in 1891 (and the company pioneered the publication of catalogs of its wares), the entry into the disc market almost coincided with that of its rival, Victor, at least under that name. For Victor, as distinct from Improved Gram-O-Phone Records, made their début in the fall of 1901, and on November 6, 1901, it was announced in the press that "Columbia are already making disc records." Legal actions supporting this and that patent were sensibly suspended, and the patents themselves were pooled, to give Victor and Columbia almost total monopoly over the disc business for the next fifteen years.

The Columbia factories and headquarters for the first eight decades or so of the company's life were located in Bridgeport, Connecticut, but are now in New York City. From both sources have come some of the most remarkable, interesting, and beautifully recorded examples of the sound engineer's art. For although early on, like most makes, Columbia surfaces were inclined to be gritty and the stout core of mica and microscopically thin rice paper all too often caused a distressing rumble, by the time electric recording had been perfected around 1926 the smoothness of the surfaces and natural recording quality of Columbia records made them outstanding for that time or any other. The introduction of the Royal Blue Record, in which an almost purple hue replaced the normal black, was not quite the commercial success its makers had hoped. The smoothness had given way to some extent to a rather rough effect, although the recording quality was unchanged.

As might be expected, pressings made under war conditions stood little chance of favorable comparison with those produced in peace time, and the popular red-label Columbias of the 1940s, and to some extent the blue-label classics of the same period, sound very gritty at times and again rumble. These defects seemed not to trouble the followers of Frank Sinatra, Doris Day, Harry James, and others at all, however, as these artists' records all sold in huge numbers. The end of the 78 was nigh, however, when in June 1948, Columbia introduced the first commercially viable long-playing records, playing at 33⅓ rpm, with tiny groove width and pressed in noiseless unbreakable vinylite. The 78 lasted another decade or so, finally being replaced by the 45 rpm "single," seven inches in diameter and made in exactly the same way as the long-playing records.

Columbia, over the nine decades since those first rough, crude cylinders that played for two minutes to excited listeners with ear tubes like stethoscopes, has been the parent company to a number of subsidiary labels. At the outset, unsold stock of Columbia pressings were sold *en bloc* to various talking machine dealers, music stores, and other firms, who resold them with their own lables pasted over the Columbia design. Among these were Aretino, Diamond, Harmony, and Standard. The name Harmony was revived in September 1925 for a new low-priced record (fifty cents compared to seventy five cents for the equivalent popular Columbia). Simultaneously, Velvet Tone made its début, using the same material as Harmony, and Diva, made for the W.T. Grant chain stores, likewise. In August 1930, a strange month at the best of times to launch a new label, and stranger still in a trade recession, Columbia announced a new thirty-five-cent label called Clarion. It did not produce exactly the same issues as its affiliates, many of the items in its catalog being issued only on Clarion. All four labels were withdrawn in June 1932.

There were other makes that were produced by Columbia. One, as far back as the beginning of Columbia's first disc issues in 1901, was known as Climax. It was apparently made *for* Columbia by the Globe Record Company, but all known issues are identical to regular Columbias of the era bearing the same numbers. The curious fact about Climax records of this date is that they bear an embossed mark of a circle surrounding the letters VTM, which must surely mean "The Victor Talking Machine (Company)," and Mr. W. Keessen of 's Gravenhage, Holland, tells me that Eldridge R. Johnson, before launching the Victor Talking Machine Company, organized a small company for producing discs, which he called the Globe Record Company.

From November 11, 1926, Columbia took over the General Phonograph Corporation, makers of OKeh records, and continued to press these, with the advantage of Columbia recording and pressing techniques. When ARC absorbed Columbia itself, OKeh was allowed to lapse into an ill-deserved oblivion, while Brunswick's associate Vocalion was fully maintained. Three months after CBS had disposed of Brunswick, it also discontinued the Vocalion identity, reintroducing OKeh and allocating the entire current Vocalion catalog to the revived mark, even maintaining the same catalog numbers. Okeh continued until well into the 1960s, although only as singles. Harmony was revived briefly in the early 1950s, and there were also a few long-players on this label. Another CBS subsidiary was Epic, but these seem to have all been microgroove issues. Other inexpensive CBS LPs include Hallmark and Realm.

In 1952, it was announced that CBS would no longer be a source of material for Britain's EMI-Columbia, and for the next twelve years or so, Philips, the British branch of the vast Dutch electrical firm, produced records, many of which were drawn from CBS. During and after the later 1960s, CBS has produced its own records in Britain.

CONQUEROR—*see* PLAZA MUSIC COMPANY

CRYSTALATE

The Crystalate Gramophone Record Manufacturing Company of Tonbridge Wells, Kent, England, once laid claim to being the oldest established manufacturers of disc records in England. Exactly which labels they produced in the years prior to World War I is not clear, but their principal interwar make is Imperial. This appeared in 1920 and continued until February 1934. It was the direct descendant of Olympic and Popular, both of which were presumably Crystalate labels.

Imperial catered to the popular market, at a popular price, and the quality of the pressings varied considerably from gritty to quite smooth. Many records from the Plaza and ARC catalogs were offered on Imperial. Shortly before the withdrawal of Imperial, Crystalate launched Rex (September 1933), having acquired the British branch of Vocalion some eighteen months earlier. Decca assumed control of Rex and Vocalion in March 1937, but Crystalate still exists as a business, though no longer engaged in producing records.

During the years from 1923 to 1937, Crystalate produced a number of labels for the dime stores of Woolworth's, beginning with Mimosa (five- and later six-inch records, 1923 to 1928); then came Victory (seven-inch, 1928 to 1931); Eclipse (eight-inch, 1931 to 1935); and finally, Crown (nine-inch, 1935 to 1937). For the rival firm of Marks & Spencer's, the six-inch Marspen record made a brief appearance in 1926 to 1927, and the Savana label, some six-inch and a few ten-inch, also came from the Crystalate factory, though the store in which they were sold is not known; perhaps they were not limited to any one particular store.

For about a year after the withdrawal of Imperial, and alongside Rex, there was a label known as Imperial Broadcast, mostly reissues of material from both these catalogs.

DECCA

The Decca label was launched in England in July 1929, and was the longest survivor of the spate of labels that appeared on the British record market about that time; most of the others had a lifespan of up to four years. Decca vanished as a label early in 1980 when Polygram, a European conglomerate, assumed control of it.

At the outset, the studios were in the Chenil Galleries in Chelsea, London, and the records made there invariably had a constricted sound that reminded listeners of the old acoustic method of recording. Sessions were also undertaken in Battersea and Chelsea Town Halls, and in another large hall in the West End of London, with much improved results. Decca records became a force to be reckoned with, and in 1933 new studios, an impressive catalog of top names in entertainment of all kinds, all at a highly competitive price helped to establish an enviable position. The Warner-Brunswick catalog was adopted, and in the summer of 1934, the American branch was set up in New York. This provided much valuable material in the form of records by Bing Crosby, the Boswell Sisters, the Mills Brothers, and many front-rank dance bands, most of these being issued on English Brunswick.

From 1933 to 1938, most Decca recording in London took place in a building in Thames Street, near the river; but after the acquisition of Crystalate's assets in the material sense, the studios in West Hampstead were used. The factory in Malden, Surrey, operated throughout Decca's half-century of life on the British record market.

Its American counterpart was originally based in New York, but now, under the auspices of the Music Corporation of America, Decca in America operates from Universal City, California. From the beginning, recording has always been done regularly in New York, Chicago, and Los Angeles, but there have been short location recordings done in New Orleans, San Francisco, and a few other locations. Never very much concerned with recordings of classical works until teh cominf of LPs and all their potential in this field, Decca nevertheless at least balanced this by producing records by top best-selling artists such as the Andrews Sisters, Judy Garland, the Ink Spots, and Bill Haley, the rock-'n'-roll protagonist who is credited with launching the craze in 1956 with his "Rock Around the Clock." It was Decca that produced the best-selling album set of the music from the 1943 Broadway hit *Oklahoma!* sung by the original cast, having bowed to the AFM demands a good year before Victor and Columbia followed.

It was Decca that in 1945 announced the newest technique in recording —"ffrr" or full-frequency range recording—and five years later launched the first long-playing vinylite microgroove issues in England. After the war, the London label was introduced in New York and, in 1949, in England; it featured many artists whose records in England had been issued on Decca with huge success. Over the years, London has issued a remarkable and varied selection of long-playing records, from classics of the concert hall to classics of jazz, and many unusual records in the sphere of currently popular artists. Decca linked the French Ducretet Thomson label with London, and for a time also issued all kinds of European recordings on the Felsted label.

Originally, and for the first quarter-century of its life, the Decca record had as its trademark a likeness in bust form of Beethoven, but he has since disappeared in favor of a stark, plain panel that simply proclaims the name of the firm. London used no design other than the word itself in italic capitals.

DEUTSCHE GRAMMOPHON

One of the largest German record companies, Deutsche Grammophon reaches back in history to the era when the original Gramophone & Typewriter Company abandoned its "angel" trademark on records in favor of the dog and brass-horn Berliner gramophone. This was in 1909; after World War I, the German branch of the Gramophone Company that produced "His Master's Voice" records had seceded from the parent firm and was producing records of its own with the famous trademark and the legend

"Die Stimme seines Herrn," but for export it was suppressed, and such expatriate pressings bore the name Polydor and a curious dehumanized figure apparently listening with a stylized ear trumpet at each side of its head!

Today Deutsche Grammophon has branches all over Western Europe, and its products on microgroove, all serious music, are a standard for excellence, artistically and technically. The dog, the Berliner machine, and the Polydor monstrosity have all gone in favor of a panel bearing the company's name in script, bordered by a row of tulips or some similar flowers. Berliner's original factory was built in Hanover in 1898, and Deutsche Grammophon's headquarters are there to this day.

DIVA—see COLUMBIA

DOMINO—see PLAZA MUSIC CO.

DUOPHONE—see BRUNSWICK

EDISON

The first successful attempt to record and *reproduce* sound was made on November 29, 1877, by Thomas Alva Edison. This much is fairly common knowledge, broadly speaking. He began marketing records as a commercial venture in the early 1890s, first on wax cylinders made in his studio in Orange, New Jersey, or in New York. By the opening years of this century, a duplicating process had been devised ("the gold-molded process") that would relieve the performers from the burden of having to record every song or piece of music over and over again until the immediate demand was met. In October 1908, a "long-playing" cylinder, scratchy but of four-minute duration in contrast to the two minutes of the earlier type, was introduced, and exactly four years later there came a much superior cylinder on almost noiseless plastic, known as the Blue Amberol.

These were on sale, regularly increased every month, until Edison decreed the end of the record business as of November 1, 1929. They were dubbed from discs that were eventually also put on the market from October 1913. Thereafter, certain Amberols, taken from the Edison Diamond Disc repertoire, were chosen for issue. Not everything made or issued on disc was automatically included in the Blue Amberol catalog.

Despite the firm association of Edison's name with electrical devices, his records were not made electrically until June 1927. The Diamond Discs were a race apart; about a quarter of an inch thick, recorded so that the track was cut vertically, and of such minute dimensions that only an Edison stylus could play them on an Edison machine, which would play no other make, it is remarkable that they lasted as long as sixteen years.

Nevertheless, Edison Diamond Discs appealed to a wide market both in the United States and in Europe, and half a century or more after their demise there are still many collectors of all kinds of recorded music who regard them as the ultimate, at any rate in acoustic recording. So interesting do they seem that Raymond Wile, of New York, was able to compile a complete account of them (see chapter 6) and produce it as a monumental major discographical work of the first importance.

A few weeks before closing the record side of the business, Edison produced a conventional ten-inch and twelve-inch lateral-cut record, of which a few specimens still exist. They do not seem to match their long-established competitors on Victor, OKeh, and Columbia either in technical quality or musical interest.

EDISON BELL

The Edison Bell Company was an all-British concern that operated roughly the first third of the twentieth century, beginning with cylinder records and graduating to discs in 1909. The quality of these was often extraordinarily good, especially in view of the inexpensive price, and the repertoire included some very ambitious works as well as the more pedestrian fare.

The factory and studios were in the London suburb of Peckham, under the personal management of a vigorous Empire-builder, J.E. Hough, who, like Edison himself, knew exactly what he liked and had no objections to expressing his taste. His business was maintained for some eight years after his death in 1925 by his family, eventually selling out to Decca, who own the rights to the trademark and some of the repertoire to this day. (Decca introduced a short-lived Edison Bell Winner series of its own in 1933; it lived two years, whereas J. E. Hough's Winners were on the market from 1912 to 1932.)

Winner was not the only Edison Bell label by any means. In 1913 the Velvet Face record was introduced, concerned mainly with music of a more permanent nature than that on Winner, and in 1927, Electron began its three-year life, devoted to the more expensive dance bands, popular artists, and serious works, similar to Velvet Face. Between the spring of 1928 and that of 1932, there was also extant the Edison Bell Radio record, eight inches in diameter, that gave excellent value for money.

ELECTROLA

This is the German equivalent of "His Master's Voice," brought into being in 1926 to offset the post-World War I loss of Deutsche Grammophon (q.v.). It continues today as a leading label for serious works, as HMV does elsewhere. The headquarters, once in Berlin, are now in Cologne.

EMERSON

Victor Emerson had been a recording engineer for Columbia in the earliest years of the century, and when the basic patents covering disc recording expired, he set up the Emerson Phonograph Company in 1916. At the beginning, Emerson records were 5½ inches in diameter, retailing at twenty-five cents each, increasing in size to seven inches, nine inches, and eventually ten inches by 1919. At one time during that year, all three sizes were on the market simultaneously, in addition to a short-lived twelve-inch series.

The postwar boom that became a bust hit Emerson's enterprise hard. Overconfidence and a recording program to rival Victor and Columbia that never fully materialized put the company into the hands of a receiver in December 1920. Production on a necessarily reduced scale continued until a creditors' meeting was held in May 1922. At the end of that month it seemed that Emerson must go under, but on June 1, two magnates in the manufacturing of phonographs came forward with an offer for the business, which was accepted.

The newly organized firm was incorporated in New York two months later, and in January 1924 a radio division was formed. The following November, the incorporators sold the record division to the Scranton Button Company of Scranton, Pennsylvania. This continued to market Emerson records, and various other lines, until the end in 1928. The Emerson Radio and Phonograph Corporation exists to this day in New York.

During the boom years of 1918 to 1920, Emerson produced such labels as Medallion, Melodisc, and Symphonola, in the same variety of sizes as the parent label. The Scranton product was of ten inches diameter only, but by no means as smooth-surfaced as its predecessors. Early in 1926, a system of electric recording was introduced, but this too was inferior to most of the cheap line competition. At the very end, a subsidiary known as the Nutmeg Record Corporation introduced the seven-inch Marathon record that lasted for a matter of weeks only.

Emerson masters have been found to have been used on such divers British labels as the unbreakable Duophone and Goodson (1927 to 1928), Edison Bell Winner, Ideal-Scala, Homochord, Beltona, Grafton, and Piccadilly. All but Piccadilly, which itself was introduced in England in the autumn of 1928 as Emerson was dying, are mid-1920s labels, evidently as a result of leasing arrangements concluded by one of the incorporators, Benjamin Adams, on a trip to Europe in 1924. The twelve-inch variable-speed World records are often dubbed from Emerson. All these labels issued their Emerson material under pseudonyms as a rule, with few exceptions indeed.

GENNETT

This label was named for the brothers Fred, Harry, and Clarence Gennett (pronounced with a soft 'G' and with the accent on the second syllable) who were the principal officers in the Starr Piano Company of Richmond, Indiana, in 1917, when it was decided to branch into the phonograph and record business. The first issues, in October of that year, were vertical-cut discs with almost microgroove dimensions. These enjoyed excellent sales for some eighteen months, then a lateral record was introduced under the same brand name. This was maintained until December 1930. The Starr Piano Company then withdrew its main label, but continued with the lower-priced Champion that had been marketed since September 1925. In December 1934, this too was withdrawn, and sold to Decca on June 28, 1935. But Decca never showed much interest in its new acquisition, and after about a year it was discontinued.

The recording studio in Richmond itself had little to commend it. It was situated close to a railroad track, which created obvious problems every time a heavy locomotive passed. Gennett maintained a studio in New York from the outset until the end of June 1932. There were also recordings made on location trips to New Orleans, Chicago, Los Angeles, Birmingham, and St. Paul.

Gennett's chief claim to fame lies in its having pioneered a large number of recordings of what is now termed "classic jazz" by such giants as King Oliver, Louis Armstrong, Jelly-Roll Morton, the New Orleans Rhythm Kings, Bix Beiderbecke, and Hoagy Carmichael. Although the system of recording them leaves much to be desired, they are nevertheless very valuable documents of their kind.

Gennett masters were available to, and used by, such British labels as Aco, Beltona, Coliseum, Edison Bell Winner, Guardsman, Homochord, Scala, Sterno, Tower, and Vocalion. Other American subsidiary labels include Champion, Superior, Supertone, and Silvertone, the latter two being issued by Sears, Roebuck & Co., through its mail order service.

GRAMOPHONE & TYPEWRITER (G & T)

The term "G & T" has long signified the label of the Gramophone Company's products prior to the move of the factory in 1908 from Hanover, Germany, to Hayes in Middlesex, England. The Typewriter was adopted as a subsidiary business venture in December 1900, in view of managing director William Barry Owen's conviction that the prosperous business would soon collapse when the novelty of the talking-machine had worn off. In fact, it was the Typewriter that failed to promote sales, but for the seven years from the end of 1900 to the end of 1970, this label has always been one of the richest hunting grounds of collectors of vocal records of the highest intrinsic worth (see chapter 6).

GREY GULL

The significance of Grey Gull records lies more in their ramifications throughout the American and, to some extent, the British market than in the quality of the music recorded and the method of recording it. The earliest Grey Gull records appeared in pre-electric days in May 1919 and lasted until the late summer of 1930. The headquarters of the firm were in Boston, Mass., and from there, records were issued on Radiex, Van Dyke, Madison, Sunrise, and Supreme in America, and on Piccadilly, Metropole, Dominion, and Goodson in England. I once attempted to list all the known details, in order of matrix numbers, but the complex nature of the products, some issued several times under different pseudonyms, sometimes anonymously, and even with alternative titles to the numbers themselves, rendered the project virtually impossible. To complete it as far as issued records are concerned, with all label and other information included, would necessitate seeing and even hearing the records! A considerable number of them, on American labels, were at one time to be found in British secondhand stores, and are known to have been sold in Woolworth's branches throughout the United Kingdom in the early 1930s.

The Grey Gull label is interesting mostly to jazz enthusiasts of catholic tastes, as it offers a wide spectrum of performances more or less in the jazz idiom amid a welter of straight dance band numbers and popular-style vocal records. The recording quality is inclined to be harsh and the surfaces, not noted for their ability to withstand rough usage, are usually noisy.

HIS MASTER'S VOICE

Some notes on this, the world's most famous label, will be found in chapter 6. Its history, with references to its repertoire, has been the feature of various books (Roland Gelatt. *The Fabulous Phonograph.* New York and London: Cassell, 1956, etc., and Leonard Petts. *The Story of "Nipper" and the HMV Picture.* Bournemouth, Eng.: The Talking Machine Review International, 1973), and there have been two books from the recording impresario's viewpoint. Both are concerned with the memoirs and biography of Fred W. Gaisberg, Emile Berliner's emissary to Europe in 1898, who remained with the Gramophone Company until shortly before his death in 1951. It was once remarked of Gaisberg that, "His middle initials shoud be H.M.V." One of these books, *The Music Goes Round*, renamed *Music on Record* for the British market, was written by Fred Gaisberg himself during World War II, and published in London (Robert Hale, 1946); the other, *A Voice in Time*, by Jerrold Moore (London: Hamish Hamilton, 1976) complements the first excellently.

From the first embryonic Berliner days, through the Gramophone and Typewriter years (both q.v.), to the present, HMV has always dominated the European and Antipodean market, with a similar coverage of the Far East and the entire Western Hemisphere by its American associate of fifty-seven years, Victor (also q.v.). A treatise on the complex numbering systems of both masters and issued records would need a volume or series of volumes of encyclopedic proportions. Reference to the booklength discographies in chapter 6 will show what attempts have been made in this direction.

His Master's Voice's subsidiary, Zonophone, was originally almost a pirate label. It was introduced in 1899 by Frank Seaman, the disenchanted publicity agent originally associated with Berliner. After the failure of his legal actions to debar Berliner from marketing his own merchandise, Seaman seems to have vanished from the scene, but Zonophone records continued to appear, probably rather sporadically, from the incorporation of the Victor Talking Machine Company on October 3, 1901, until the Gramophone and Typewriter Company in England, and Victor in America, bought the Zonophone concern out in July 1903. Thereafter, for about eight years in America and nearly thirty in Britain and Australia, the name was used as a second string to the bow of the giants who dominated the world market. Prior to 1903, Zonophone in various countries in Europe had produced some very desirable operatic items, now of legendary rarity. In England, in later years, it was in the forefront of the jazz producers, but in America its repertoire consisted mainly of the usual commonplace ballads, light instrumental numbers, and comedy songs. After the formation of EMI Ltd. in England in 1931 between HMV, Columbia, and Parlophone and their subsidiaries, it was only a matter of time before Columbia's inexpensive subsidiary, Regal, and HMV's Zonophone were "married" to form a single label. From January 1933, Regal Zonophone continued to offer a high-quality product, technically and aesthetically, as each of the contracting parties had been offering for twenty or more years.

HOMOCHORD

The Homochord (or, as its German originators spelled it, Homokord) record is one of some significance as a British label, as it derived its often interesting catalog from various European sources prior to World War I in 1914, and from such American origins as Gennett, Emerson, Vocalion, Pathé, and even Victor during the 1920s. Pre-1914 issues, most of them recorded in London, were pressed in Germany and exported to Britain. From the autumn of 1921 until the end in the summer of 1935, the British Homophone Company marketed them, but the pressings came from the Vocalion factory in Hayes, Middlesex, the Pathé factory in Stonebridge Park, London, and—from 1926 to 1928—the Gramophone Company's factory, also in Hayes. From 1928 to 1935, Homophone made their own pressings in their Kent factory.

During the time when Vocalion pressed Homochord records, the latter drew not only on American and English Vocalion masters for their monthly supplements to the catalog, but did a considerable amount of recording in London in their own studio. There was modicum of the more serious kind of music included in the catalog, but most of the repertoire was devoted to dance music, popular vocals, and light instrumentals. The Victor masters were used during the two years when Homochords were being pressed by the Gramophone Company. Little is known of the extent of this curious interrelationship, but as Victor masters were used on Zonophone, and Homochords called on Zonophone artists for their British recordings during the 1926 to 1928 period, the connection becomes a little clearer.

IMPERIAL—see CRYSTALATE

LINDSTRÖM

Carl Lindström was the owner of a large record manufacturing empire during the 78 rpm era. Its products, centered in Germany, included such labels as Beka, Odeon, Fonotipia, and Lindström itself, later adding Parlophon (which became Parlophone in English in November 1923). The General Phonograph Corporation in New York, makers of OKeh records, q.v., was the American outpost of the Lindström empire.

Beka and Lindström records were never sold in the United States under these names, but Odeon (q.v.) and Fonotipia were. The Società Fonotipia di Milano was originally an independent concern, devoted to the making of beautiful records of many of the world's finest singers, violinists, piano soloists, and actors. These became part of the Lindström combine just before the outbreak of World War I. Fortunately, many of the original masters were preserved by Parlophone until the late 1930s, when each month would see the issue of a coupling from the Fonotipia repertoire. Their diameters were ten and three-quarter inches or twelve inches, and their quality was superb. Columbia entered into an agreement with the

Società in 1910 in an effort to secure some top-grade singers not already contracted to Victor or its overseas affiliates. The project was not out-standingly successful.

The amalgamation of HMV, Columbia, and Parlophone in 1931 seems to have brought the Lindström régime to an end. OKeh in America had been a Columbia subsidiary since the end of 1926, and with it, Odeon. High-grade products continued to appear under all the various labels except Lindström itself, however, and the Odeon mark, never used in England except in conjunction with Parlophone, was revived there on its own by EMI in 1978.

METROPOLE

This was a short-lived but high-grade label sold in England between the spring of 1928 and sometime in 1930. Its subsidiary, Piccadilly, costing half the price but of almost as fine quality, first appeared some six months after Metropole and lasted until April 1932. Much of what was issued on Metropole was also released as Piccadilly, under various pseudonyms, and a considerable number of Emerson and Grey Gull masters were im-ported from America and used for both labels. All are ten-inch records. Mostly designed for the popular taste, Metropole issued some sides of music composed and conducted by Sir Edward German, while its low-priced affiliate offered a slightly higher-priced celebrity record on which appeared such interesting items as the British composer Joseph Holbrooke playing his own piano pieces. The head office was in Finsbury Square, London, E.C. 2, and the studios, evidently very well-equipped if the sound recorded there is any criterion, were in the same building.

M-G-M

The Hollywood film company of Metro-Goldwyn-Mayer entered the disc market soon after World War II, and rapidly became known as a major force in the record world. Many recordings from film soundtracks have been issued, both as 78s and LPs, including songs by film stars, some of whom have made no other commercial records, and incidental music. Although classical concert music was well-represented in America on M-G-M, the European catalogs were largely confined to popular issues (mostly vocal, with a proportion of modern concert orchestras, and little real jazz or dance music, as both were considered to be of little commercial value when M-G-M launched a record division of the film company). From the beginning of 1948 until the early 1970s, EMI handled M-G-M records in Europe, but since then, the affiliation has been with Polydor, q.v.

ODEON

An important subsidiary of Lindström, q.v., Odeon records began their career in France and Germany as long ago as 1904. The trademark is truly international, as examples of Odeon records, bearing the stylized "temple" design, can be found in Turkey, Japan, Malaysia, throughout Europe, South America, and the United States. They are notable for the high quality of their manufacture, recording technique, and a repertoire catering to all tastes on a grand scale.

OISEAU-LYRE

This important connoisseur's label designed for those interested in serious works, especially those by little-known but interesting composers, has been produced in France from the mid-1930s on. It is manufactured by the Pathé-Marconi branch of EMI in Paris, and as a result has superb technical qualities to match the excellence of its catalog.

OKeh

The principal product of the General Phonograph Corporation of New York, under the management of Otto Heinemann, OKeh records were originally vertical-cut when first put on sale in September 1918. About a year later they became lateral-cut, and went on for seven years to produce some of the finest examples of acoustic recording of all time (and from a jazz and blues enthusiast's viewpoint, some of the truly great classics in both idioms).

There were OKeh catalogs devoted to each of many languages during this time, and these are treasure houses of rare folk music. As was noted in the section on Columbia, that label took over the production of OKeh records at the end of 1926, and for nine more years the two makes provided some of the most delightful records that matched in all aspects their predecessors of the acoustic era. Revived in July 1940 by CBS, OKeh continued through to the microgroove years. Although it is to this day a subsidiary of CBS in the United States, a special clause in the agreement between Lindström in Germany, Parlophone in England, and the General Phonograph Corporation in America provided that OKeh records were to be issued in England only on Parlophone, who as a label had sole rights to the OKeh masters permanently.

Because of the superb quality of the music on OKeh records, and that of the system used to perpetuate it, the compilation of a complete file of OKeh recordings by matrix mumber has long been the dream of several discographers, myself included. The rarity of many of them, however, has slowed the project down to a virtual standstill. Through the courtesy of CBS, I can trace anything and everything made by or for OKeh during the Columbia era. However, the files of the General Phonograph Corporation have been severely diminished by time and various changes of address over the years, therefore, the kindness of collectors possessing actual copies of the records and willing to share the information on them is my main source of material. OKeh records of any kind rarely show up in English secondhand stores, and I always welcome hearing from anyone who can and will impart even so much as the details of one OKeh issue that has so far eluded me.

ORIOLE

In America, this was a very inexpensive label designed for the McCrory chain of stores from 1921 to 1938. Its catalog was drawn from Emerson and the Plaza Music Company's repertoire, later known as American Record Corporation. As might be expected, it was aimed at the less wealthy members of the public who felt that a quarter was quite enough to spend on a couple of dance tunes or popular songs.

In England, three Oriole labels, all produced by the music store of Levy's in London's East End, have appeared between 1927 and 1950. The first batch was of fourteen issues in two sections in May and June 1927, almost all devoted to top-grade jazz and blues items from American Vocalion's "race" catalog. These vanished quickly, and are now some of the rarest and most sought-after British-made jazz issues. Between 1931 and 1935, a second series of Orioles was produced rather sporadically, again very jazz-oriented, but using American Mercury and Tempo masters as well as British recordings from sessions arranged by Levy's. The third, more catholic in its appeal, made its début in 1950, and it continued through the following decade, enjoying many vast-selling successes on 78s and LPs alike. The quality of recording is very good. It is not known why the name was chosen for any of the British issues, since there is no sign on any of them of the Maryland bird, which in any case is not known in England.

PANACHORD—see DECCA

PARAMOUNT

Although the firm that produced Paramount records was called the New York Recording Laboratories, Inc., its executive office was in Port Washington, Wisconsin, where it was established in 1916. Recording was carried out in studios in New York and Chicago, and later in Grafton, Wisconsin.

Little attempt was ever made in the sixteen years of the label's life to interest lovers of serious music. Instead, Paramount tried to capture the burgeoning clientele of black Americans able to afford a machine and records in the post-World War I boom years. They succeeded in this, and today Paramount enjoys a position of special importance among blues aficionados. (See chapter 6 for details of Max Vreede's book on the Paramount "Race" Series.)

There were other records issued as well, but most of these were dance and popular vocal items, with a smattering of light instrumental fare. Paramount provides a curious and unusual example of a label on which the acoustic recordings are generally superior in quality to the electric. The earlier types are usually excellent, and pressed on good quality shellac, but the latter often have noisy, abrasive surfaces even when seldom used, and the sound quality is usually inferior to that of the major labels, although the price asked was the same (seventy-five cents).

Paramount masters were obviously available to many other record companies, such as Plaza Music Company, Emerson, Black Swan, and (in England) Imperial. Recordings made by Plaza, and by Orlando R. Marsh in Chicago, appear on Paramount freely from 1925 to 1929, and there is evidence toward the end of some association with a short-lived popular-styled label called Crown. There were a number of Paramount subsidiaries during the 1920s: Broadway, Claxtonola, Puretone, Puritan, and Triangle are among those most frequently found.

PARLOPHONE

The principal interwar representative in Britain of the Lindström-Beka-Odeon-Parlophon combine in Germany, Parlophone first appeared in November 1923, and rapidly progressed to the forefront of British labels. Its American affiliate, OKeh (q.v.) having been absorbed by Columbia in November 1926, Parlophone followed suit in England in 1928, and was thus one of the founding fathers, so to speak, of the vast EMI combine that also included HMV and Columbia itself.

During the 1920s, Parlophone was one of the labels that supplied masters for the north-country store of J.G. Graves of Sheffield, Yorkshire, which used them on its Ariel records, usually under a bewildering variety of pseudonyms. These continued to appear until a year or two before the outbreak of World War II, but a complete listing of them has yet to be found or compiled. Certain items that have been found on Ariel, with Parlophone or OKeh masters, do not appear to have been issued on such labels. Anyone can be forgiven for speculating as to what else, perhaps in the nature of collectors' desiderata, may have been released with an Ariel label.

PATHÉ

For many years, Pathé was the principal label in France, for it sold at a price below that of its Gramophone and Columbia competitors. The fact that the records (introduced in October 1906, twelve years after the first cylinders) had to be played with a ball-tipped sapphire stylus fixed in the soundbox, instead of steel needles that tiresomely needed changing after each playing, no doubt helped to strengthen their popularity. The earliest issues had no labels, the details being etched as expeditiously as possible in the central area in an arc surrounding it. Labels were introduced during World War I, following the opening of a studio in New York.

The founders of Pathé Frères Pathéphone were Charles and Emile Pathé, joint owners of a bistro in Paris. Having experienced an Edison cylinder phonograph at a trade fair in Vincennes, they were convinced that the installation of something similar in their establishment would be of great commercial value—as it was. The cylinders were abandoned during World War I. The discs came in the strangest and most outlandish sizes (eight and one-half, eleven, fourteen, and even twenty inches in diameter), and played at 90 rpm.

After World War I, although the original vertical-cut system was retained, a so-called needle-cut (that is, lateral-cut) disc known as Pathé Actuelle was introduced in both America and Britain. It lived as a moderately good seller until the end of 1928 in Britain and March 1930 in America. In December 1928, Columbia bought Pathé's British branch, and during the 1930s French Pathé records were produced by Pathé-Marconi. The quality of the recording, which had been shrill when acoustic and cloudy, rather lacking in definition when electric, now reached the normal high standard of a Columbia product.

America introduced the subsidiary Perfect in July 1922, and this was retained after American Pathé was absorbed by the American Record Corporation, up to the discontinuation of many "shoestring" labels in April 1938. For the most of their existence, Pathé Actuelle and Perfect synchronized their issues. What appeared on one at seventy-five cents appeared on the other, Perfect, at fifty cents, then thirty-nine cents, or three for a dollar. Pseudonyms between the two labels were the exception rather than the rule.

PERFECT—see PATHÉ

PHILIPS

The vast Dutch electrical firm began issuing records only as 78s were being phased out, and it launched on the British market in January 1953. For some twelve years, it promoted CBS records in Europe, but CBS having declared independence, Philips has since issued items from other sources. The present distributor in England is Phonogram Ltd., in London. The principal subsidiary label is Fontana.

The Philips catalogs represent all kinds of music to suit all tastes.

PICCADILLY—see METROPOLE

PLAZA MUSIC COMPANY

This firm launched into the record business in New York in 1921, and over the next fourteen years its principal label, Banner, was popular with those wishing to obtain their favorite dance tunes or popular songs at a price commensurate with their pockets. Banner made its bow in January 1922. To begin with, its repertoire drew from such labels as Emerson and Paramount, both q.v., but from early 1923, Plaza began recording in its own New York studio, continuing this until the merger of Cameo, Pathé, and the Plaza group in 1929.

The Plaza group included such labels as Domino, Oriole, and Regal, and a very similar, but not identical repertoire appeared on all of these, sometimes under the same artist credit and sometimes in a general switch-round of identities. Domino apparently had a source of masters entirely its own, because they do not bear Plaza-series matrix numbers and are not to be found on any label but Domino as far as extensive research has so far shown. They did not last long. Domino records continued to be issued up to 1932, however, under the American Record Corporation's aegis.

POLYDOR—see DEUTSCHE GRAMMOPHON

PYE

Pye has long been established in the forefront of British radio and television, but it was not until 1955 that the company went into the record business. It took over the small semiprivate company known as Nixa, and for about five years produced 78s of quality along with some excellent LPs. For a short time the company marketed the American Mercury label in England.

QRS

The QRS Piano Roll has been established since the first decade of the twentieth century as the finest quality product of its kind. In 1923, with the help of the Starr Piano Company and its thriving Gennett catalog, QRS issued a few records that did not prove very successful, apparently, as they are exceedingly rare today. Five years later, in the Gennett studios in Woodhaven, Queens, New York, QRS made a number of recordings that were independent of Gennett itself, and intended only for issue on QRS. (Several were also issued on Paramount later.) Again, these are very rare; they consist principally of excellent "hot" jazz, blues, and country music.

After about a year, a new series of QRS records, recorded and manufactured by the Cova Recording Corporation in New York City, made a brief appearance. Some were actually issued in England on Goodson (q.v.). They were designed for a more catholic taste, and included dance music and popular vocal items. They do not seem to have lasted beyond 1930.

REGAL

American Regal records were on sale from the spring of 1921 until the latter part of 1931. They relied mostly on Plaza Music Company masters, although for the first year or so Emerson supplied some, and Paramount others. When the American Record Corporation weeded out some of its string of labels in 1931, Regal was one to be discontinued. It was a cheap popular-style brand and, during its life, very prolific and welcomed heartily by the public for which it was intended.

The British Regal was also an inexpensive line, produced by Columbia from the spring of 1914 until December 1932, when the EMI merger brought about a liaison with HMV's less expensive label, Zonophone (see HMV). Both types of record had a wide appeal throughout their lifetimes, and like American Regal, they presented the appearance and sound of a top quality article at a very low price. At one time, from 1935 to 1937, Regal Zonophone cost 1 s., the equivalent then of about twenty cents. At no time were Regal or Regal Zonophone records priced higher than the sterling equivalent of fifty cents, the price of an American Regal at the outset.) The Regal Zonophone label continued in production until November 1949. In the 1960s, it was revived briefly for a number of popular LPs.

REX

Like Regal, there have been two labels of the same name, Rex, in America (1912 to 1916) and Britain (1933 to 1948). The American brand is an insignificant vertical-cut affair manufactured by the Rex Talking Machine Corporation of Wilmington, Delaware; the British one was originally the principal label of the Crystalate Gramophone Record Manufacturing Company, q.v., of London, until Decca took over in March 1937. Its catalog was geared to match that of Regal Zonophone, but although the recording quality was excellent, the surfaces were less durable.

SOCIETA FONOTIPIA DI MILANO (FONOTIPIA)—see LINDSTRÖM

STERNO

Like Homochord (q.v.), Sterno was a product of the British Homophone Company of Tunbridge Wells, Kent, England. It featured much the same repertoire, and extended it to edited versions on eight-inch records bearing such brand names as Solex, Plaza (no connection with the New York Plaza Music Company), Lewis, and Peacock. The Gramophone Company of Hayes, Middlesex, pressed Sterno records from the summer of 1926 to the summer of 1928. After this, a new series was introduced, pressed briefly by Pathé (q.v.), and subsequently by British Homophone itself. In the summer of 1937, EMI and Decca between them bought the assets of British Homophone as far as their issuance of records was concerned, and thus over the next three years or so, Sterno masters were used occasionally to supply items for the Decca and Regal Zonophone catalogs. The only known American connection with Sterno is through its Homochord affiliation much earlier with Gennett and, afterwards, Vocalion. Most Sterno records are ten-inch, aimed strictly at the popular taste, but there was a brief attempt to attract a more cultured market with a series of twelve-inch popular classics.

TELEFUNKEN

This was one of the principal German labels during the late 1920s through the war years. (In Czechoslovakia, its subsidiary was known as Supraphon, and in France as Ultraphon.) They were manufactured by Telefunkenplatte GmbH, Berlin, and like the majority of German pressings, have superb surfaces and beautiful recording characteristics. They catered to every kind of German taste, even occasionally including such non-Aryan fare as jazz, but concentrated on serious works, often recorded complete. After the end of World War II, there was a brief series of issues in England on a Telefunken label, manufactured by Decca. Most of these were of serious works, with some examples of excerpts from operettas.

USSR

The State label of Soviet Russia is of considerable interest in that its catalog offers unusual material by Soviet artists and composers not met with elsewhere as a rule. The overwhelming majority of USSR records are of Russian material, of course, and as far as I know, there is no Western popular music of any kind to be found on them. The first issues seem to date back to the 1920s, and their covers state that they were pressed in the factory at Aprilevka, the source of Russian G & T and HMV records in prerevolutionary times. The quality is excellent.

During World War II, Decca secured the rights to a selection of USSR records, which proved very popular with British customers.

V-DISC

The official issue of the United States War Department during World War II, V-Discs first appeared in 1943. They continued as regular Armed Services issues until 1948, always twelve-inch, sometimes pressed in vinylite, sometimes much more solidly made in laminated form like CBS Columbias and OKehs. The vinylites were usually pressed by Victor and the others by CBS. The featured artists were all top-liners in serious and popular music alike. Some of them made their contributions especially for V-Disc, while others were represented by dubbings from discs already issued commercially. Sometimes the artist would speak a message at the beginning of the side, thereby adding a certain value to the record as being the only recorded example of his or her speaking voice.

Although the records were intended for use by service personnel only, once they had been distributed to all the fighting units in Europe, Asia, and Oceania, there was little or nothing that could be done to prevent their changing hands in return for civilian favors, human nature being what it is. Unused copies of records for which this or that unit did not care would command quite good prices, and many are preserved today in pristine condition.

After it was considered that they had fulfilled their official purpose, no further issues were made, and the masters were scrapped in the presence of various service chiefs and a news cameraman who dutifully recorded the melancholy scene. The artists involved in the making of V-Discs did so without fee or royalty payment on the strict understanding that their work would not be used for commercial purposes. This being so, their union could have no objection to what would otherwise have been a form of strikebreaking, as many of the recordings made for V-Discs were carried out during the "Petrillo ban" on members of the American Federation of Musicians recording for normal commercial purposes.

VELVET FACE—*see* EDISON BELL

VELVET TONE—*see* COLUMBIA

VICTOR

America's best-known and longest-established *disc* record has been referred to many times in this book in connection with its Berliner and Improved Gram-O-Phone predecessors, but there is this to add. Like HMV, Victor's affiliate label from 1901 to 1957, Victor records appeared in much the same format in many countries. Usually the very catalog numbers are the same, whether the actual pressing was done in the United States, Canada, Brazil, Chile, Argentina, Japan, or China, and in Canada there was also a "His Master's Voice" label resembling the Victor in every detail except for the absence of the name. This HMV species was reserved for local Canadian talent and imports from Great Britain that were not issued on Victor elsewhere. The domestic Victor catalogs show records made by the company in dozens of languages, each with its own catalog series.

As was mentioned in chapter 6, I had begun some years ago to compile a discography of at least the domestic black-label records designed by Victor for popular consumption. What is needed as a true picture of the extent of Victor's recording activities over the years is a complete account of everything from the beginning to at least the end of the 78 era. There is a special need for this, as Victor made a practice of not divulging the all-important matrix numbers on their records, nor yet on the labels, contrary to the procedure of almost all other companies, large and small. Before the spring of 1906, however, this detail was shown, etched by hand on the run-off; after this it disappeared until the spring of 1928. For about six months after that date, the matrix number appeared on both the record and the label, only to vanish again until 1953, since when it has been given its place on wax and label. It is hoped that such an encyclopedic work can and will be produced eventually. As an historical document it would be unsurpassable.

It was Victor that pioneered the long-playing record, as long ago as September 1931. Ten- and twelve-inch discs, some single-sided, were issued in considerable numbers in the following three years, but during those particular years when economic conditions did not favor costly items such as records, even fairly inexpensive 78s, sales were not encouraging, and the project was abandoned. The grooves were not as miniscule as the present-day LPs, and the material on which they were pressed was a rather coarse plastic known as Victrolac, but for all the shortcomings of these rather rugged pioneers, the fact remains they were a far-sighted step in the direction the entire industry was to head—seventeen and more years later.

From the date of its incorporation on October 3, 1901, until its absorption by Radio Corporation of America on January 4, 1929, the Victor Talking Machine Company was the official name of the world's mightiest phonograph business. After that date, the records were produced by the RCA Victor Division of the corporation. The only company that Victor ever bought up was the renegade Zonophone, in July 1903. No record-producing organization has ever taken Victor over, and it is the only major label of which this can be said. It pressed records for Columbia early on (see Columbia), and in 1930 and 1931 it began pressing Crown and Gem records and a label of its own known as Timely Tunes. The latter, and Gem records, did not survive for more than a few months; Crown lasted until 1933. In 1932, Victor began producing records for the five-and-ten chain stores. There were three new labels: Bluebird, Electradisk, and Sunrise. The first issues of Bluebird were eight-inch discs, but they soon expanded to the more normal ten-inch size and, of the three, they alone went on to become the best quality product of all the thirty-five-cent labels produced anywhere. Electradisk and Sunrise vanished after just a year. Bluebird continued until March 1950, but was reactivated briefly in 1976 as an LP featuring reissues of vintage jazz and dance music. During the 1950s, Victor toyed briefly with a popular-style label called Vik, and there was also a series of vintage reissues on the X label. This was initially LPs only, but there were also a number of 78s of popular material of the day issued in 1954.

The principal pressing plant for years was in Camden, New Jersey, but there have been and still are others all over the nation. More recently the headquarters of the Record Division has been in Indianapolis. Recording sessions have been held in many cities and small towns, in the course of talent-spotting expeditions that have taken place since the introduction of electric recording (Victor called it "orthophonic") in the spring of 1925.

Emile Berliner, on his way home from a visit to Europe in May 1900, stayed briefly in London and saw the famous "His Master's Voice" trademark for the first time. He made arrangements for its use on his publicity material and, when the legal wrangles over patents had been settled and Eldridge Johnson and Berliner had successfully launched the Victor Talking Machine Company, it was only a matter of a few months before the fox terrier and the brass-horn machine became a feature of the label of every Victor record. (The trademark was also used on Bluebird from early

1939.) It was not represented in natural color, however, until the early 1950s, and after the secession from HMV in March 1957, it was eventually dropped altogether in favor of the legend RCA, in large letters suggesting those used by a computer, and the word Victor in small, lower-case type. It was revived in 1978.

As we have seen, Victor masters were used outside the Western Hemisphere and certain Far Eastern countries, on "His Master's Voice" records under this name and suitable translations, and on Zonophone and sporadically on Homochord (in England). Victor also supplied pressings to Montgomery Ward, the mail order house, under the name of the firm.

VOCALION

The Aeolian Company of New York City, piano manufacturers, began issuing records in 1916. They were vertical-cut, and playable only on Vocalion machines (and those that had been suitably adapted), but in January 1920 the first lateral-cut issues appeared, and proved very popular. In the summer of 1925, after establishing a catalog and quality of recording that compared most favorably with Victor, OKeh, and Columbia in both areas, Vocalion was taken over by Brunswick and continued as an inexpensive subsidiary to Brunswick until July 1940.

When Warner Brothers, the film company, assumed control of Brunswick in April 1930, Vocalion was accepted along with them, and when Brunswick was absorbed into the American Record Corporation in 1931 so was Vocalion. When CBS took over ARC in December 1938, both Brunswick and Vocalion were ultimately discontinued. As we have seen, Brunswick was phased out in favor of Columbia, but Vocalion simply assumed the identity of Columbia's former subsidiary, OKeh, even to using the same catalog numbers.

In England, Vocalion records have always been lateral-cut. They were launched in December 1920 and, like their American counterpart, offered a high-class product that featured some of the world's leading artists. When the merger between Brunswick and Vocalion took place in America in 1925, the English branch drew from Gennett for about a year and a half, and in the autumn of 1927 the English Vocalion label was discontinued. The company did not go out of business, however, but thrived on an eight-inch record named Broadcast from July 1927 until Crystalate adopted Vocalion in the spring of 1932.

During the seven years of Vocalion's life in England, there were a number of other labels that were affiliated with it, or, more correctly, with its slightly less expensive subsidiary, Aco. From the Aco catalog the following British labels drew their repertoire, all aimed at the popular market and featuring dance bands (many from American Vocalion), light vocalists, instrumental soloists, military bands, and comedy sketches: Beltona, Coliseum, Guardsman, Ludgate, Meloto, and Scala.

In May 1936, the Vocalion name, and a slightly modernized version of its original beautiful label, was brought back into use by Crystalate for its Swing Series, consisting entirely of records ostensibly designed for the jazz connoisseur. Six months later, an expensive popular record, the Vocalion Celebrity Series, began; this lasted about two years and was never a great success. The Decca recipients of the rights to Vocalion maintained it until February 1940. Then in October 1951 Decca reintroduced Vocalion as a means of issuing classics of jazz in a readily recognizable form. After three years, during which time only forty-one issues appeared, this too was withdrawn. In the 1960s, a Vocalion label devoted to modern "pop" made a brief appearance, and in 1977, for one issue, so far, Vocalion was revived as yet another all-jazz label.

ZONOPHONE—*see* HIS MASTER'S VOICE; VICTOR

7

A Bibliography
of Booklength
Discographies

THE CONTENTS of this chapter do not pretend to be exhaustive. I freely admit that included are only the booklength discographical works with which I am familiar. At the moment of writing, however, a start has been made on a series of books by Michael Gray, Music Librarian of the Voice of America, and Gerald D. Gibson, Assistant Head of the Recorded Sound Section of the Library of Congress in Washington. Volume 1, devoted to the classics, lists discographies of composers and artists in this field published between 1925 and 1975. Volume 2 will cover jazz; Volume 3, popular music; Volume 4, ethnic and folk music; and Volume 5, general discographies of music, label listings, speech, and animal sounds. The series, called quite simply *Bibliography of Discographies*, is being published in New York by R.R. Bowker & Co.; volume 1 was published in 1977.

The authors pay tribute to the pioneer work done in 1962 in the British Institute of Recorded Sound quarterly magazine, *Recorded Sound*, by Carl Bruun and John Gray, and later work by Lewis Foreman and David Cooper. In view of the minute documentation of known discographical books already published, my own efforts below seem very small fry, but I dare to hope that this chapter will prove of use and interest to discographers and students of recorded sound, at least pending the publication of the remainder of the incredible work of Messrs. Gibson and Gray.

I am not including the myriad of so-called discographies, many of them no more than listings drawn from whatever catalogs were available to the compiler, which have appeared in many specialist publications over the past fifty years. Nor do I include the often more useful results of true devotion to the subject matter, included as appendices to biographies of such divers artists as violinist Fritz Kreisler, opera singer Enrico Caruso, crooner Al Bowlly, and jazz cornetist Bix Beiderbecke, which I have discussed briefly in the preceding chapter.

In this chapter, I have tried to describe as accurately as I can the style and contents of each work and to assess its value as a book of reference. Obviously, normal civilized demeanor precludes my assessing my own works in this manner, so in such instances, I have merely given an outline of what each work contains and, incidentally, what it omits. Several books included will be found to have been commented on in one or more of the preceding chapters, but completeness demands that further references to them be made. Therefore, here again I am summarizing their aims and contents for ease of reference. If I have omitted any booklength discography, I apologize most sincerely both to the author and to those whose interests he serves.

Allen, Walter C. *King Joe Oliver* (Stanhope, N.J.: privately, 1955, 1956; London: Sidgwick & Jackson, 1959). Referred to at the time of publication as a "disco-biography," this is presented in the form of a biography of Joe Oliver, New Orleans-born black jazz cornetist, composer, and bandleader, with a third of its length devoted to the biography and the rest to a minute documentation of the artist's known records, with all reissues at all speeds, and notes on how the personnels of the various bands were obtained. Appendices of titles, musicians mentioned in the text, catalog numbers, and a "rarity" index are included. Illustrated, 224pp.

Allen, Walter C. *Hendersonia* (Stanhope, N.J.: Jazz Monographs, 1973). Another minutely documented account of the life and career of a black musician—pianist, arranger, composer, and bandleader Fletcher Henderson—with discographical contents interleaved, so to speak, with biographical and itinerary notes and narrative. Appendices on exactly similar lines as those in *King Joe Oliver* are included, with long-playing and other microgroove records included. Illustrated. 651pp.

Barazzetta, Giuseppe, Giancarlo Testoni, and Arrigo Polillo. *Enciclopedia del Jazz* (Milan: Messaggerie Musicali, 1954). A four-part survey of jazz in Italy, a third of the total volume being devoted to a discography of jazz records issued there, including those actually recorded in Italy. The other two-thirds comprise a glossary of terms used in jazz, an outline history of the music with considerable detail on many points, and an alphabetical directory of many musicians with useful biographical notes, entirely in Italian. Illustrated. 518pp.

Bauer, Roberto. *Historical Records* (Milan: Martucci, 1937; rev. ed., London: Sidgwick & Jackson, 1946). The standard directory to recordings made between 1898 and 1908-1909 (with a few excursions into more recent years) by prominent operatic and concert singers, on lateral-cut records only. Each artist is documented with a code-letter showing whether he or she is known to have made records for various individual companies (for example, Victor, Columbia, Fonotipia, other lateral-cut labels, Pathé discs, cylinders, Edison) and/or electric recordings. Most dates of birth and death are shown, and, in many cases, the date and place where the artists made their débuts. If they recorded an aria from an opera in which they created the role sung on the record, this is noted by the letters "CR." Although records known to have been made in certain years are listed, usually with the location, under those years, no attempt is made to show the exact date of recording, except in very isolated instances, and matrix numbers are shown for only a very few artists' records. A few pages at the end are devoted to a selection of speech records by outstanding poets and actors of the same era, ten pianists, thirteen violinists, and two cellists, and a listing of five allegedly complete operas recorded between 1906 and 1909. There is also a foreword giving brief information on seven labels most often met with in the book. 494pp.

Bennett, J. R. *voices of the Past* Series (Vol. 1: *HMV English Catalogue, 1898-1925*; Vol. 2: *HMV Italian Catalogue, 1898-1925*; Vol. 3: *Dischi Fonotipia: A Golden Treasury*; Vol. 4: *The International Red Label Catalogue, Book 1: HMV 'DB' 12-inch Series*; Vol. 6: *Book 2: HMV 'DA' 10-inch Series, both 1924-1956* (both with Eric Hughes); Vol. 7: *HMV German Catalogue* (with Wilhelm Wimmer); Vol. 9: *HMV French Catalog* (Lingfield, Surrey, England: Oakwood Press, 1955-1970). Facsimile typescript booklets of numerical listings of all traceable vocal records on the labels specified. (The English catalog comprises five actual booklets, includes not only serious vocal records but also popular, musical comedy, and music hall issues.) Composers are invariably included. Some dates of recording are shown rather sporadically, and nearly all the dates of issue are given for the single-sided element, not for the double-sided. As a basis for a discography of any kind of vocal art, these books are invaluable, but they should not be taken as being absolutely complete. Despite the painstaking efforts of the author to include every vocal record ever announced on HMV, Berliner, and associated Continental labels, some have eluded him. Matrix numbers are shown somewhat more generously than dates, but mostly of single-sided issues. Each volume lists the artists by surname only, and fully in the attendant index. Average length of each individual volume is about 300pp.

Bredevik, Gunnar. *Ulla Billquist* (Stockholm: Kungliga Biblioteket, 1970). Detailed numerical discography of a prolific Swedish popular singer, with title index. In this case, the matrix numbers are used numerically, with the catalog numbers—where there were any—shown on the right of the page; in other words, a completely professional discography. Duplicated single-sided pages. 58pp.

Chilton, John. *McKinney's Music* (London: Bloomsbury Book Shop,

1978). Subtitled *A Bio-Discography of McKinney's Cotton Pickers*, this booklet is an account of the career of the famous black jazz orchestra, including a fully professional discography. Fully illustrated. 68pp.

Connor, D. Russell, with Warren W. Hicks. *B.G. on the Record* (New York: privately, 1958, new ed., Arlington House, 1969). The standard discography of clarinetist Benny Goodman (subtitled *A Bio-Discography of Benny Goodman)*, interleaving a detailed account of his career in music with all traceable recordings, documented in minute detail as to the personnel of each band, and the audible part played by Benny Goodman himself. As usual with discographies of jazz musicians, composers are not shown in the discography itself, but a title index includes these, and all information regarding radio broadcasts known to exist on discs and tape is given. There are also artists' and radio and film indices, and a listing of records at one time believed to have been made by Benny Goodman but which have since proved not to be so. Illustrated. 691pp.

Creighton, James. *Discopaedia of the Violin* (Toronto: University of Toronto Press, 1972). A detailed account of all known violin solo records, up to the date of publication, in the field of classical works. These are arranged by artist, showing some matrix numbers, but no exact recording dates, and the work is cross-referenced by composers. 987pp.

Daniélou, Alain. *Catalogue of Recorded Classical and Traditional Indian Music* (Paris: UNESCO, 1952). Self-explanatory straightforward listing. 236pp.

Davies, John R. T., with Roy Cooke. *The Music of Fats Waller* (London: Century Press, 1950; 2nd ed., 1953). An excellent detailed discography of a world-famous jazz pianist, vocalist, composer, and bandleader. All regular discographical details given, except the recording locations, with title index. Lithographed on glossy paper. Illustrated. 40pp.

Davies, John R. T., with Laurie Wright. *Morton's Music* (Chigwell, Essex, England: Storyville Publications, 1968). A valuable essay in discography, devoted to the records and piano rolls made by Ferdinand "Jelly-Roll" Morton, Creole pianist, composer, and bandleader. It includes actual musical notations of those parts of his records of which two different takes were issued, showing the differences in such a way that even those unable to read music can distinguish them. 40pp.

Deakins, Duane D. *Comprehensive Cylinder Catalogues:* Part 1: *Cylinder Records* (Stockton, Calif.: privately published in facsimile typescript, 1956, 17pp.; 2nd ed., enlarged, 1958, 35pp.); Part 2: *Edison Standard Records* (Stockton, Calif.: privately published in facsimile typescript, 1957, 104pp.); Part 4: *Indestructible Records* (Stockton, Calif.: privately published in facsimile typescript, 1960, 36pp.); Part 5: *U.S. Everlasting Non-Breakable Records* (Murphys, Calif.: privately published in facsimile typescript, 1961, 25pp.) Part 1 of these booklets is subtitled *A description of the numbering systems, physical appearance and other aspects of cylinder records made by the major American companies, with brief remarks about the earliest American companies and the foreign manufacturers.* This is self-explanatory. The titles of the other volumes in the series describe their contents, which are documented numerically, showing as much detail as can be traced regarding each, but without exact dates or locations.

Delaunay, Charles. *Hot Discography* (Paris: Le Hot Club de France, 1936; 2nd ed., 1938; 3rd ed., 1943; 1st American ed., 1940, using the photocopied 2nd ed. for the most part, but with newly set chapters on some artists, such as Jelly-Roll Morton, by Walter E. Schaap and George Avakian); *New Hot Discography* (New York: Criterion Books, 1948). For many years these were the standard discographical reference works on "hot" jazz, as distinct from ordinary dance music. A general description of them is given in chapter 4. 626pp.

Doner, M. H., with James Cameron. *Standard International Discography of Pipe Organ Records* (Winona, Minn., and London: 1950) Although this single-sided duplicated typescript is hardly a book in the accepted sense—it has no covers and the pages, numbered with subletters and totaling about 52, are stapled together—this compilation of some 450 recordings by all kinds of pipe organ records made in the United States and Europe before 1950 is still, as far as I can trace, the only reference work of its kind. It is barely a discography in the professional sense, being more of a listing of the artists, their recorded titles, and the makes and catalog numbers of the records, without dates or any other numerical details, or, as a rule, more than one issue per title. For anyone wishing to have a ready guide to 78 rpm records of pipe organ music, or perhaps a foundation on which to build a true discography of the subject, however, this is invaluable.

Elfström, Mats. *Scala* (Stockholm: Kungliga Biblioteket, 1967). A highly professional numerical listing of all Swedish Scala records, with exact label details, most recording dates, or at least rational estimates of these where not traceable, subsequent or precedent issues, and an artists' index. Duplicated single-sided pages, illustrated. 83pp.

Elfström, Mats, with Björn Englund. *Ultraphon* (Stockholm: Kungliga Biblioteket, 1968; 2nd ed., 1976.) Similar style of numerical listing to the above, with title and artist indices. Duplicated single-sided pages, illustrated. 21pp.

Englund, Björn. *Durium/Hit of the Week* (Stockholm: Nationalfonotekets Diskografier, 1967). A numerical listing in full discographical detail of the weekly issues of the flexible Durium record, with its affiliation to the American Hit of the Week label, 1930 to 1932. No indices and no cover. Duplicated single-sided pages, unnumbered. 14pp.

Englund, Björn. *Sonora I (8000-serien)* (Stockholm: Kungliga Biblioteket, 1968). Exactly the same format as the foregoing works by Sweden's most prolific discographer. There is an artists' index, but the only illustration is one specimen Sonora label on the first page. Duplicated single-sided pages. 15pp.

Englund, Björn. *Sonora II (Swing-serien)* 2nd ed. (Stockholm: Kungliga Biblioteket, 1974). Exactly the same format as the last above, but although this is devoted to Swedish jazz records (actual or alleged) on the Sonora label, no personnels are given. Duplicated single-sided pages. 38pp.

Englund, Björn. *Sonora IV (E-5000, 6000, 9000, K-8500-serien)*. (Stockholm: Kungliga Biblioteket, 1968). Another in the Sonora series, but illustrated with six photo offsets of various kinds of Sonora labels. Artists' index. Duplicated single-sided pages. 35pp.

Englund, Björn. *Evert Taube*. (Stockholm: Struwwelpeter Gesellschaft, 1969). A professionally produced discography of a prominent Swedish popular singer who recorded from 1921 to 1954. A title index and numerical listing are shown as appendices, and even the playing time is given in most cases. Double-sided facsimile typescript. 20pp.

Englund, Björn. *Sonora VII (7000-serien)* (Stockholm: Kungliga Biblioteket, 1972; 2nd ed., 1974). Continuation of the previous series, in exactly the same format. Illustrated with four photo offsets of the Sonora Elit variety of label. No indices of any kind. Duplicated single-sided pages. 70pp.

Englund, Björn, with Tage Ringheim. *Svenska violinister på Skiva (1907-1955)* (Stockholm: Kungliga Biblioteket, 1973). Discography by artist of recordings made by Swedish violinists between the dates shown. Composers' and numerical index; short biographical notes on the majority of artists, in Swedish. One label illustration. Duplication single-sided pages. 42pp.

Englund, Björn. *Telefunken* (Stockholm: Kungliga Biblioteket, 1975). Numerical listing of Telefunken records by Swedish artists, fully documented with artists' index and seven label illustrations. Duplicated single-sided pages. 47pp.

Englund, Björn, with Lars-Göran Frisk. *Musica* (Stockholm: Kingliga Biblioteket, 1976). Numerical listing of Musica records, fully documented with artists' and title indices, and seven label illustrations. Duplicated single-sided pages. 127pp.

Englund, Björn. *Sonora IX (Outgivna inspelningar)* (Stockholm: Kungliga Biblioteket, 1977). Incomplete but remarkably well-documented listing by matrix number, with dates and usual discographical details, of Sonora records from 1932 to 1958. Artists' index. One label (test sample) illustration only. Duplicated single-sided pages, closely typed. 23pp.

Englund, Björn, with Bo Gäfvert. *Ragnar Sundquist and Sven Hylén.*

(Stockholm: Kungliga Biblioteket, 1977). Chronological listing of all known recordings by the above-mentioned Swedish piano-accordionists. Title index, numerical reference. One Sundquist label illustrated only. Duplicated single-sided pages, with fullest discographical details. 38pp.

Englund, Björn. *Roulette/Triola* (Stockholm: Kungliga Biblioteket, 1978). Numerical listing of these two Swedish labels, with fullest details. Artists' and title indices. One label of each make shown on first page. Duplicated single-sided pages. 38pp.

Flower, John. *Moonlight Serenade* (subtitled *A Bio-Discography of the Glenn Miller Civilian Band*) (New York: Arlington House, 1972). Minutely documented chronological account of the formation of the Glenn Miller band, with all known records (including composers). Radio programs and films included; times of regular recording sessions shown. Details given of *Metronome* Dance Band Polls, artists' and title indices. Lavishly illustrated, a discographical masterpiece. 554pp.

Fraser, Norman. *International Catalogue of Recorded Folk Music* (London: International Folk Music Council and Oxford University Press, 1954). Volume 4 of Series C (Archives of Recorded Music) prepared for UNESCO. Listed by country or continent, subdivided by language (for example, African tribal songs listed as AFRICA—Bantu, Swazi, etc.) or by description if given section is all one language. No dates or matrix numbers, titles, short descriptions, and artists shown in that order. 201pp.

Fribourg. *Catalogue du disque de musique religieuse* (?Paris: UNDA [Association internationale pour la radiodiffusion et télévision], 1956). I have not been able to examine a copy of this work, which comprises 300pp.

Girard, Victor, with Harold M. Barnes. *Vertical-cut Cylinders and Discs* (subtitled *A catalogue of all "Hill-and-Dale" recordings of serious worth made and issued between 1897-1933 circa*) (London: British Institute of Recorded Sound, 1971, original ed., 1964). A magnificent production in double-sided pages of facsimile typescript, concerning artist listings with as much detail of date, location, and matrix number of every known record coming within the limits imposed by the title. Not only are all vocalists other than music hall and cabaret artists included, but also instrumental soloists of repute. Obviously dance records, jazz, and light orchestral and military band items do not qualify, but most of these are covered elsewhere. There are many pages devoted to the identification and numbering of cylinders and Pathé recordings of all kinds, and two appendices: A, devoted to complete operas and plays, of which Pathé enterprisingly produced a large number, and B, a numerical listing of anonymous Pathé recordings of vintage 1897-1900. (There are four columns of these, closely typed). Hard cover, embossed. Six etched-label Pathé illustrations. 234pp.

Godrich, W. J., with Robert M. W. Dixon. *Blues and Gospel Records,*

1902-1942. (London: privately published, 1963; 2nd ed., Chigwell, Essex: Storyville Publications, 1971). A most valuable discography of all known records of blues singers and "gospel" performers (that is, Negro sacred singers, soloists and in groups, as well as preachers with and without congregational support) recorded within the very sensibly chosen time limits. Artists are listed alphabetically, with fullest detail of numbers, locations, dates (including the day of the week when the exact date is known), and original 78 issues. Rejected titles are of course included where known, as are recordings of relevant material made by the Library of Congress sound archive division. LP numbers are not shown, but where a 78 rpm record is known to have been issued on a microgroove recording of any speed, this is indicated by a small "m" immediately before the matrix number. These two editions are out of print at this writing (1979), but a third is expected to be published by Storyville in 1980. 912pp.

Gronow, Pekka. *American Columbia Scandinavian "E" and "F" Series* (Helsinki: Finnish Institute of Recorded Sound, 1973). A chronological listing by catalog number of all records coming within the scope of the title, showing many matrix numbers and takes, but no dates, and otherwise full details. Some dates of issue are shown. Double-sided pages, facsimile typescript, with interesting quotations from publicity material of the time of the original issues. Two illustrations from Columbia supplements. 130pp.

Gronow, Pekka. *Studies in Scandinavian-American Discography I* (Helsinki: Suomen Äänitearkisto, 1977). A comprehensive listing of all known American issues of performances recorded there and elsewhere by Scandinavian and Finnish artists. Listed by make, then numerically by catalog number, with almost all matrix numbers, takes, and many recording dates. Some composers shown. Much front matter on the foreign-interest catalogs, generally of the principal American makes of 78 rpm records. Copiously illustrated with facsimile labels, contemporary publicity material, and so on. 112pp.

Haapanen, Urpo. *Catalogue of Finnish Records*. 13 vols. (Helsinki: Suomen Äänitearkisto, 1976). Covers, collectively, 1902 to 1976 and includes two alphabetical indices (Vol. 9 and 10); Volume 1, 1946-1966 is out of print at the time of writing.

Hayes, Jim. Five booklets covering each of the following subjects: *Edison Bell 8-inch Radio 800 Series, 1928-1932; Crown 9-inch, 1935-1937; Brunswick (English), (0)1000-02000 series, 1930-1935; Decca (English) F-1500-F-3999, 1929-1934; Edison Bell Winner W-1 series, 1933-1935.* Numerically arranged by catalog number, many matrix numbers, but no dates of recording. Duplicated typescript, published by author.

Hurst, P. G. *The Golden Age Recorded* (Henfield, Sussex, England:

published by the author, 1946; subsequent ed., London: Sidgwick & Jackson). Of the 175 pages comprising this book, the only discographical part is a 43-page appendix devoted to certain selected singers arragned in vocal categories (sopranos, contraltos, tenors, baritones, and basses), and then subdivided alphabetically, giving the same information as Bauer (q.v.), in almost exactly the same format (no exact dates, no matrix numbers, no takes or locations). The preceding part of the book deals with biographical details of the artists and others, whose records are not included in the appendix, however, as well as chapters on collecting early vocal records, the early years of the gramophone itself, the principal labels on which operatic and other vocal rarities were issued, and some notes on speech, instrumental, and comic records of the same era as covered by the vocal section (1902-1908).

Jasen, David. *Recorded Ragtime, 1897-1958* (Hamden, Conn.: Shoestring Press, 1973). A first-class listing of ragtime music, shown under title, composer, and artist, with all known recordings of any one composition shown under its title, with original record numbers (no matrix numbers, no locations, and recording dates given to a month and year, the year being shown first in abbreviated form). Ten labels illustrated. Lithograph. 155pp.

Jepsen, Jorgen Grunnet. *Jazz Records, 1942-1962* (some volumes extend to 1965, a few to 1967) (Holte, Denmark: Karl Emil Knudsen, 1963-1969). Twelve volumes, presenting details of jazz records made within the time limits given in the title. Personnels, locations, many matrix numbers, few takes, many exact dates, but many blanks. Facsimile typescript, double-sided pages, paperback binding that tends to crack and loosen the contents. Average 400pp. per volume.

Karlsson, Kjell-Åke. *Åke Grönberg.* (Stockholm: Kungliga Biblioteket, 1976). A discography of a Swedish popular singer, presented entirely professionally in the same format as those in the same series by Björn Englund and/or Mats Elfström (q.v.). Matrix numbers, takes, locations, dates of recordings, all issue numbers, title index, numerical index, one (Sonora) label illustration. Duplicated typescript, single-sided pages. 26pp.

Kendziora, Carl. *The "Perfect" Magazine* (New York: Record Research, 1963). A numerical listing of all issues on the Perfect label, dance band series, 1922 to 1930. Titles, composers, artists, issue dates, some recording dates, nearly all matrix numbers and takes, with history of the Perfect label. Illustrated with many valuable and unique photographs and photo offsets. 48pp.

Lange, Horst. *Die deutsche "78er"—Discographie der Jazz—und Hot-Dance Musik 1903-1958* (Berlin: Colloquium Verlag Otto H. Hess, 1966). The definitive manual on jazz records made in or issued in Germany in the period described by the title. Arranged by artist, it shows all the necessary discographical details for a work of this kind, many of them being published only in this book. 775pp.

Lange, Horst. *The Fabulous Fives* (Chigwell, Eng.: Storyville Publications, 1978). Another model discography, omitting nothing whatever from the visible and audible aspects of all the records included in it: the small (mainly five-piece) pioneer jazz bands of the early and middle 1920s. Copiously illustrated with rare photographs of the bands, their publicity material, record labels, and so on, with such interesting and unusual features as an index to label illustrations and a sales-figures list for Columbia issues. 150pp.

Liliedahl, Karleric. *Sven-Olof Sandberg* (Stockholm: Kungliga Bib-Numerical catalog showing full details of all known recording on this Swedish label. Artists' index, five label facsimile illustrations. Single-sided duplicated pages. 51pp.

Liliedahl, Karleric. *Dacapo* (Stockholm: Kungliga Biblioteket, 1969). Similar style of production to the above; artists' index, one label facsimile illustration. Duplicated single pages. 23pp.

Liliedahl, Karleric. *Ernst Rolf* (Stockholm: Kungliga Biblioteket, 1970). A fine discography, arranged correctly, showing all known records by a Swedish popular singer who recorded for many labels from 1910 to 1932. Ten label facsimile illustrations, title and numerical indices. Duplicated single-sided pages. 75pp.

Liliedahl, Karleric. *Sven-Olof Sandberg* (Stockholm: Kungliga Bib-lioteket, 1971). Exactly the same format as the foregoing, covering the records of another popular Swedish singer, from 1927 to 1959. Title and catalog numerical indices, no illustrations. Duplicated single-sided pages. 72pp.

Liliedahl, Karleric. *Dixi/Silverton.* (Stockholm: Kungliga Biblioteket, 1972; 2nd ed., 1974) All known records on these Swedish labels listed by matrix number, covering all correct details for a professional discography. Four label facsimile illustrations. Title and artists' indices. Duplicated single-sided pages. 113pp.

Liliedahl, Karleric, with Frank Hedman and Lars Zackrisson. *Alice Babs* (Stockholm: Kungliga Biblioteket, 1973). Excellent discographical essay on the records of a favorite Swedish popular singer, recording from 1939 to 1973. Full details of usual necessities. Only illustration is fron-tispiece photograph of the artist herself. Title and numerical label indices. Duplicated single-sided pages. 87pp.

Liliedahl, Karleric. *Harry Brandelius* (Stockholm: Kungliga Biblio-teket, 1975). Exactly same format as for any of the above, but artists' and numerical catalog listing only. Duplicated single-sided pages. 58pp.

Liliedahl, Karleric. *John Forsell* (Stockholm: Kungliga Biblioteket, 1977). Valuable discographical essay on "one of Sweden's foremost singers," as the preface (in English) describes him. Titles, composers, and label indices. One facsimile label illustration. Duplicated single-sided pages. 26pp.

Lord, Tom. *Clarence Williams* (Chigwell, Essex, England: Storyville Publications, 1976). First-class model discography of a prolific and most important jazz personality, with indices covering artists, biographies, titles, LPs, and so on. Hardcover. 625pp.

Mahony, Daniel. *Columbia 13/14000-D series* (Stanhope, N.J.: Walter C. Allen, 1961). Numerical listing of the two Columbia "race" series of 1923 to 1933, with full details of label copy, recording and issue dates, pressing figures, artists' and title indices. Double-column layout on each page. Double-sided facsimile typescript. Twelve label facsimile illustrations. 80pp.

McCarthy, Albert, with David Carey. *Jazz Directory* (Fordingbridge, Hampshire, England: Delphic Press [Vols. 1-4], 1949-1952; London: Cassell [Vols. 5-6], 1955-1957). Unfinished discography of all kinds of records of jazz and music more or less associated with it, including blues, ragtime, gospel singers, sermons, dance bands of certain types, and popular singers with jazz accompanists. Letters A-Lo covered in some detail; many matrix numbers (few takes), some exact recording dates (few locations). Excellent format, well-printed (lithograph) on good quality paper. (See chapters 3 and 4 for more detailed assessment.)

Moses, Julian Morton. *Collectors' Guide to American Recordings* (New York: American Record Collectors' Exchange, 1949). Numerical listing of vocal celebrity records issued in the United States on Victor, Columbia, and others between 1895 and 1925 (the acoustic era). 200pp.

Pernet, Robert. *Jazz in Little Belgium* (Brussels: Editions Sigman, 1967). Fully professional discography of jazz musicians recording in Belgium, or of Belgian origin recording elsewhere, with full details. 150 illustrations, artists' and titles indices, bibliographies, history of jazz and kindred music in Belgium (in French). Hardcovers. 518pp.

Prieberg, Fred K. *Musica ex machina* (Berlin: Ullstein, 1960). Lists records of electronic and experimental music, musique concrète, music for new instruments, film music, and modern music generally, according to Carl Bruun and John Gray (*A Bibliography of Discographies*, in *Recorded Sound*: summer 1962, p. 208).

Robertson, Alex. *The Apex 8000 Numerical* (Pointe Claire, Quebec, Can.: published by the author, 1971; rev. 1974). Numerical catalog of Apex 8000 series records (dance music and popular items, 1923 to 1929), with matrix numbers, most takes, titles, and artists. Duplicated typescript, single-sided. 58pp.

Robertson, Alex. *Canadian Gennett and Starr Gennett 9000 Numerical* (Pointe Claire, Quebec, Can.: published by the author, 1972). Exactly the same layout as the foregoing. Duplicated typescript, single-sided. 30pp.

Robertson, Alex. *Canadian Compo Numericals* (Pointe Claire, Quebec,

Can.: published by the author, 1978). Numerical listing of Canadian Crown, Domino, Apex, Minerva, Melotone, and Sterling records produced by the Compo Company of Lachine, Quebec, during the years 1929 to 1942. Matrix numbers, almost all take numbers, titles, artists, and links with other labels all shown in meticulously tabulated columns, exactly the same as the previous works by the same author. Issue-date span shown at the foot of each duplicated typescript page; single-sided. 87pp.

Roe, L. F. MacDermott. *The John McCormack Discography* (Lingfield, Eng.: Oakwood Press, 1972). Alphabetical listing by title of all John McCormack records, showing composer, accompaniment, catalog and matrix numbers with takes; exact dates for all Victor and HMV records made in and after 1910. Unissued items listed separately at the back of the book, separating Victor from HMV, followed by numerical listing of double-sided issues on these labels, separating ten- from twelve-inch. No illustrations other than one of the singer on the card cover. Printed in reduced facsimile typescript. 93pp.

Ruppli, Michel. *Atlantic Records.* Vols. 1-4 (Westport, Conn.: Greenwood Press, 1979). An exhaustive listing in a total of close to 1,500 pages of all but the very few first recordings made by or for Atlantic Records from 1947 to 1978. Typescript, clear and easily referable, and every entry is shown in strict numerical order of matrix number. This, and the companion volumes on Prestige and Savoy records by the same author and publisher, must be regarded as absolute monuments of discographical literature. It would take a bold, omniscient genius to be able to fault them.

Rust, Brian. *Jazz Records, A-Z, 1897-1931* (Pinner, Middlesex, England: published by the author, loose-leaf limited edition, 1961); *Jazz Records, A-Z, 1897-1931,* as last, hardcover binding, omitting blues records, 1963; *Jazz Records, A-Z, 1932-1942,* extension of last, 1965; *Jazz Records, A-Z, 1897-1942,* combination of last two, (Chigwell, Eng.: Storyville Publications, 1971; 2nd ed., New York: Arlington House, 1978). 2 vols., 1,996pp. Discographical survey in fullest detail (omitting LP numbers unless a given title, recorded at 78 rpm, has only appeared in LP form), with matrix and take numbers, titles, issues, rejects, fullest known personnels, locations, and many exact dates for all known ragtime, jazz, "swing," "hot" dance, and vocal records accompanied by jazz musicians. Artists' and title indices. Composers shown for ragtime titles only. Photo offset from typescript.

Rust, Brian. *The Victor Master Book, 1925-1936.* Vol. 2 (Pinner, Middlesex, England: published by the author, 1969). Numerical listing by matrix number of all Victor recordings on domestic black-label series, Bluebird, Timely Tunes, Electradisk, and Sunrise from the beginning of electric recording to the end of the series of matrix numbers then extant.

The last take made on any session is shown. Catalog numbers are listed in an appendix with the relevant matrix numbers, as Victor products rarely show the latter. Artists' and title indices. All details of instrumentation, location, and exact recording date as shown in the original files of RCA Victor are included. Photo offset from typescript. Hardcovers. No illustrations. 776pp.

Rust, Brian, with Edward S. Walker. *British Dance Bands, 1912-1939.* (Chigwell, Essex, England: Storyville Publications, 1973). Discography modeled on *Jazz Records* (see above), for all known recordings of British dance bands between the years mentioned in the title, omitting the bands that were engaged for recording purposes only. (This book is now out of print, but a future edition is planned, which will include all British dance bands of any kind within the time limits.) No indices or illustrations. Reduced photo offset from typescript. Hardcover. 460pp.

Rust, Brian, with Allen G. Debus. *The Complete Entertainment Discography* (subtitled *from the 1890s to 1942*) (New York: Arlington House, 1973). Discography modeled on *Jazz Records*, with biographical notes on most of the artists, who consist of American-born stars of stage, screen, radio, and cabaret, or other nationals well-known in the United States. LP numbers shown where applicable, up to 1972. Only illustration is of Alice Faye, due to a defect in the pagination in the middle of her chapter. Hardcovers. Photo offset from typescript. 677pp.

Rust, Brian. *The American Dance Band Discography, 1917-1942.* 2 vols. (New York: Arlington House, 1975). Discography modeled on *Jazz Records*, with self-explanatory title. Only 78 rpm records listed. Artists' index. No illustrations. Hardcovers. Photo offset from typescript. 2,066pp.

Rust, Brian, with Rex Bunnett. *London Musical Shows on Record, 1897-1976* (London: General Gramophone Publications, 1977). Tripartite work giving chronological listing of the first nights of every musical production staged in London between these dates, with asterisks denoting those from which any number has been traceably recorded, whether by the cast or not; an alphabetical listing of the shows with any recordings, giving theater, opening night, general description, book, words and music writers, cast, and recordings of noncast artists in full discographical detail, and a discography of all artists ever appearing in any musical production, giving (with few exceptions) complete details of all their recordings, whether of titles from productions or not. LPs shown where these are the only known recordings. No illustrations. Hardcovers. Photo offset from typescript. 672pp.

Rust, Brian. *Discography of Historical Records on Cylinders and 78s.* (Westport, Conn.: Greenwood Press, 1978). Alphabetical listing of speakers (statesmen, politicians, divines, sporting personalities, and others) in

English, who recorded commercially on cylinders and 78 rpm records from the 1890s to the 1950s. Much biographical detail given in chronological tables. LPs shown where these are the only published recordings. No illustrations. Hardcovers. Photo offset from typescript. 327pp.

Rust, Brian. *British Music Hall on Record* (London: General Gramophone Publications, 1979). Discography of music hall personalities, based on the style of *Jazz Records*, with full details, from the beginning of recording to the 1950s and 1960s and the gradual, but ultimate demise of the music hall as a form of public entertainment. No illustrations or indices. Hardcovers. Photo offset from typescript. 301pp.

Schleman, Hilton R. *Rhythm on Record* (London: The Melody Maker [now Odham's Press], 1936). Alphabetical listing of many American and British (and some European) jazz and dance band personalities, with a large number of sometimes rather inaccurate personnels, some biographical details, many excellent illustrations. No matrix numbers or takes; only one catalog number for each entry. Two-column layout to each page, lithograph. Artists' index. Hardcovers. 333pp.

Smith, Michael. *The Catalogue of D and E His Master's Voice Recordings* (subtitled *The Black Label Catalogue*). (Lingfield, Surrey, England: Oakwood Press, 1961). Numerical listing of the entire black-label series of HMV records, comprising those artists considered at the time to be of more exalted status than those of the "popular" plum-label series (B and C prefixes), but less so than those of the red labels (DA and DB series). Some matrix numbers and dates shown. Facsimile typescript. 148pp.

Stagg, Tom, with Charlie Crump. *The Revival Negro Bands and Musicians of New Orleans, 1937-1972* (Chigwell, Essex, England: Storyville Publications, 1974). Entirely professional discography of the material indicated in the title. Artists' and title indices. Hardcover. 340pp.

Strömmer, Rainer. *Olavi Virta Discography* and *Georg Malmsten Discography* (Helsinki: Finnish Institute of Recorded Sound, ? 1972). I have not been able to inspect either of these works.

Triggs, W. W. *The Great Harry Reser* (London: Henry G. Waker, 1978). Detailed discography of all known recordings made by American banjoist Harry Reser, solo and accompanying, and with many bands. Arranged by make of records, but makes are not in alphabetical order. Chronological listing within each make chapter. Much valuable comment and quotations from musical periodicals. Profusely illustrated with photographs of Harry Reser himself, his various bands, publicity material, sheet music covers. Hardcovers. 200pp.

Vreede, Max E. *Paramount 12/13000 Series* (Chigwell, Essex, England: Storyville Publications, 1971). Numerical listing, including most matrix numbers and take numbers, of all known issues in the "race" series of records produced by the New York Recording Laboratories on their Paramount label between 1923 and 1932. For the most part, the listing occupies the righthand page only; the left side is illustrated by photo offset excerpts of Paramount advertisements from *The Chicago Defender* during those years. Eleven illustrations of Paramount label variations in full color; title and artists' indices, referring to the catalog numbers of the records instead of the pages, which are not numbered. 236pp.

Waters, Howard J., Jr. *Jack Teagarden's Music* (Stanhope, N.J.: Walter C. Allen, 1960). Bio-discography in paperback form of jazz trombonist Jack Teagarden. Full discographical details shown, composers excepted. Films, non-Teagarden recordings, titles, artists, catalog numbers, LPs listed in appendices; also itinerary of Teagarden's professional engagements, 1920 to 1960. 231pp.

It should be understood in connection with the foregoing that my references to "a professional discography" imply that fullest details of each entry are given, that the book is not simply a collection of extracts from a number of catalogs. The absence of such a description does not mean that the work concerned is not professionally produced. Indeed, most of them, particularly those dealing with jazz and dance band personalities, are fully professional in that they show the majority, if not all, the matrix numbers, likewise the takes, all titular and numerical data relative to the issue of the side, the location, and at least an intelligent, knowledgeable assessment of the date of recording if it is not known exactly. I have tried to convey the quality of each work of reference in the general description of it.

In my own discographical work, I have attempted to standardize the the abbreviations for labels and instruments and associated terms. (Vocal abbreviations seem to me unnecessary, as there are usually only five types of voice, and listing these in full takes little space anyway.) I have never been able to understand why it was originally considered necessary to define the country of origin of a record by applying an abbreviation for the name of the country to the make, e.g., PaE (for English Parlophone), CoF (French Columbia), HMVAust (Australian HMV), and so on, when the catalog number itself, with any prefix letters it may have, supplies the nationality. Still less do I understand why a French HMV, described on the label as "Disque Gramophone" *and* "La Voix de son Maître," should be rendered as GrF. (Presumably, the Italian HMV, labeled "Disco Grammófono" and "La Voce del Padrone," should logically be entered as GrIt, which is hardly the most complimentary of implications regarding the surface of the record. Instead, it is usually indicated as VdP; yet a Spanish HMV is described as GrSp, not VsA—La Voz de su Amo—as we are surely entitled to expect.) All that is needed in these cases is for the original title of the trademark, His Master's Voice, to be shown as HMV, and the

French designation then becomes K or L, say, the Italian R or S, the Spanish AE, the Australian EA, and so on.

Further, I have attempted to establish a label abbreviation that bears a closer resemblance to the full name of the record make than the customstaled forms of the past forty years and more. Thus, Vic for Victor, not Vi; Har for Harmony, not Ha; Par for Parlophone, not Pa (PA is my logical abbreviation for Pathé Actuelle); VT for Velvet Tone, not Vel, which could as easily denote Velvet Face (VF); Col, not Co, for Columbia (Clm being Coliseum); and so on. Similarly, I have never been satisfied with the abbreviations used to denote instruments: tpt for trumpet seems a waste of space when t will serve. (Likewise tb is all that is necessary for trombone, not tbn or even tbne, as I have seen, nor even trom.) Some discographers use cel for violoncello (I use vc, the initials of the two parts of the word), but this could—and as far as my own work is concerned, does—indicate celeste. Others use all kinds of contrivances for this, such as clst, cls, and cels. I dislike pf for piano; admittedly, if vc means violoncello, then pf means pianoforte, but how much simpler to call it simply p! (Pf is at least an improvement on pno or pfte.) Other discographers vary their abbreviations for the guitar (g is surely quite sufficient), one school using gui, another gtr. I do not attempt to distinguish between the various types of brass bass horns; tuba or sousaphone, helicon or serpent, I shorten them simply to bb (brass bass). This does not mean that the various other horns are all lumped together, for I use ah for alto horn, bh for baritone horn, th for tenor horn, and eu for euphonium. Some discographers use the term db for the string bass (sb is my term here), meaning double bass, but I suggest that db is a useful shorthand form for "doubling" (playing more than one instrument on a session, or even on a single title). The clarinet is another instrument for which I have encountered a variety of unsuitable forms of abbreviation. Cl is my preference; I have seen clt, clar, clari, and clart, some of which are barely abbreviations at all. Wo and po for Wurlitzer organ and pipe organ respectively look faintly ridiculous; I use simply or for any kind of organ not dependent on electricity entirely, the electric species being designated elo, which is neat and quite *elo*quent enough for its purpose. Elg for electric guitar also seems adequate, by the same token. For instruments and makes of record occurring very infrequently, I use the full word as a rule; to abbreviate ophicleide, sarrusophone, viol da gamba, and jews-harp seems to be creating unnecessary difficulties for the reader, much as does the use of all the symbols ever devised (the dagger, the double dagger, the two parallel lines, the curly interlinked s-like devices, the paragraph sign, and, worse, a motley combination of several of these). A discography is intended as a work of reference, after all; it should be one of easy reference, and practices such as these only create clutter, confusion, and probably to some extent chaos.

One other curious anomaly lies in the case of the earliest European labeled products of the erstwhile Gramophone & Typewriter Company and its successor, the Gramophone Company. The picture of "His Master's Voice" by the late Francis Barraud was painted in 1899, sold to the Company when its products were still graced by the name Berliner. This picture was never used on its labels until 1909, and the caption not until the following year. From the end of 1900 until the beginning of 1908, the trademark of an angel sitting on a record, apparently marking the groove with a large quill pen, was captioned by the name of the company as "The Gramophone & Typewriter Ltd., and Sister Companies." Surmounting this, around the upper rim, were the words "Gramophone Record" (for seven-inch discs), "Gramophone Concert Record" (for ten-inch), and "Gramophone Monarch Record" (for twelve-inch). (Dame Nellie Melba's records were known as "Gramophone 'Melba' Records" and Adelina Patti's as "Gramophone 'Patti' Records," but these were exceptions.) From January 1908 until February 1909, the same design, but with the caption "The Gramophone Company, Limited, and Sister Companies," was in use. For many years such records have always been known by the rather absurd term "Pre-dog." When the dog and gramophone eventually appeared on the labels, and for exactly eighteen months thereafter, the surmounting brand name remained the same as before; the term "His Master's Voice" did not come into use until August 1910. If a record is labeled "Gramophone Concert" or "Gramophone Monarch," that is, or should be, sufficient description in itself. The nature of the trademark, be it a celestial being or a homely fox terrier, is immaterial. If we are going to classify records in a discography by the exact name of the parent company, then surely all Bluebird, Sunrise, Timely Tunes, and Electradisk records should be noted as merely Victor; at least certain Zonophones should be called HMV (they bear the dog and gramophone trademark, after all), and so on. If a Gramophone Concert/Monarch record remained currently available long enough to be pressed with a "His Master's Voice" label, its entry in a discography could be resolved thus: GC (or GM)/HMV; otherwise, GC or GM should suffice. The fact that contemporary French pressings by "La Cie. The Gramophone & Typewriter Ltd. et Sociétés Filiales" are described as "Disque Pour Gramophone" does not necessitate any new abbreviations or symbols, at least for discographers writing in English, because the records themselves are international in their numbering. A French, Italian, German, Spanish, or any other nationality of Gramophone Company product bears the same number in all countries as it does in its own, until the coming of double-sided records in 1912 with a single catalog number. Double-sided "angel" label issues—and some "dog" labels—prior to this date were frequently issued in Europe, although not in Britain, but they bear the same catalog number on each side they would have borne if they had been single-sided, and no number is common to both sides.

In most discographies, the most important figure is the artist, and as a result, comprehensive works list their contents alphabetically by artist, with a title index if necessary. In a vast enterprise such as *World Encyclopaedia of Recorded Music*, obviously the composer is of prime importance, and students seeking knowledge of what works of which composer have been recorded, and by whom, are not likely to be in the least interested in the matrix number, the take, or even the exact date of recording (although a more orderly presentation of the material under each title, and less reliance on symbols, would have made for easier reference, surely). It is not at all easy to understand why certain discographies of vocalists are presented alphabetically by title, with all kinds of cross-references where variants of some titles occur from issue to issue. A title *index* is very desirable, even essential, but in a work focusing on the recording by a certain artist or group of artists, those artists should surely command pride of place. The principal objective of a discography, as distinct from a catalog distillation, is to present a chronological account of the work of an artist to enable comparisons between how the artist sounded at the outset of his or her career and years later, to display the changes in style, if any, and the expansion of repertoire. An alphabetical listing cannot serve any of these objectives.

It is saddening, even deplorable, that in years gone by the written records of some recording companies should have been lost or destroyed as waste paper and that copies of historically *and* artistically important records should have been wantonly consigned to the scrap heaps to make foundations for motorways (and during the war to fashion instruments of death). Despite this, collectors and discographers are performing valuable tasks in building permanent monuments to culture before it falls irrevocably into the hands of twentieth-century vandals.

APPENDIX I

Glossary of Terms Used in Discography

AS WITH every science, there are terms used in discography and the pursuit of collecting records, chiefly 78s, that are unique or that have totally different meanings in this connotation from their meanings in other contexts. The following are those most often met with in discographies and treatises on discographical subjects.

ALTERNATIVE TAKE. When a record company holds a recording session, it is usual for several "takes" to be made of one particular performance, rather like several shots being taken of the same subject in a photographer's studio or of the same sequence in the making of a film. Today, with the universal use of tape that can be edited, the various attempts by the artist, complete or not, can be collated as one composite "take," but in the days when wax blocks were used for recording, it was necessary as a rule to make at least two recordings of each performance in case anything went amiss with the one chosen to go into production. Quite often, some unforeseen technical problem would arise: the master providing the positives, and thus the negative stampers used for pressing, might break up in processing and be rendered useless, necessitating the use of a different master performance of the same title. Then again, having selected a certain take for issue, there might be second thoughts among members of the selection committee or even the artist himself or herself as to the suitability of this take. All these contingencies might arise after the first chosen take was already in production. In this case the second choice would go on sale, in addition to the first, as an *alternative* to it. In the case of a huge popular success, more than one perfect take would be chosen and put into production from the outset, in a desperate attempt to keep abreast of demand. One take which provided more copies than others, would become regarded by collectors and discographers as the regular example of that recording, and any variation would thus become *the alternative take.* (For some strange, unaccountable reason, many collectors and discographers illiterately term this "the alternate take," which is, of course, nonsense; alternate takes would be numbered 1, 3, 5, or 2, 4, 6, and so on, obviously.)

BUCHMANN-MEYER EFFECT. These two German physicists discovered during experiments with sound recording in the 1920s that, if a beam of light is thrown onto a disc record, the grooves produce an effect suggesting the branches of a Christmas tree, with the root at the last groove. They further discovered that the length of the "branches" is in direct proportion to the amount of sound recorded in that particular groove or grouping of grooves, and that the brightness and clarity of definition of the "branches" is also in direct ratio to the brightness and clarity of sound from the relative grooves. Thus, a record depicting a sharply defined image of a Christmas tree will give an excellent performance, no matter how improbable this might seem from a cursory examination of its surface in normal or subnormal light. And, if part of the "Christmas tree" image is dull and the rest bright, the bright part will provide an excellent reproduction of the recorded sound. A record giving only a vague, blurred outline, barely recognizable as a Christmas tree, will thus give only a very poor reproduction; and some records have been found with the grooves so badly worn by constant playing with blunted needles or styli, probably with heavy pickups or soundboxes, that they are almost ground smooth and give no Christmas tree (Buchmann-Meyer) effect at all.

CATALOG NUMBER. As the term implies, this is the number under which a record appears listed in the catalogs, leaflets, and other publicity material issued by the company owning the rights to it. This number is common to both sides of the record and appears on the label (except in the case of some early Odeon and affiliated makes such as Jumbo in England) and sometimes in the smooth part surrounding the label. (The Odeon and Jumbo issues show the catalog number only in the wax around or under the label.) In the case of single-sided records in the earliest days, the catalog number often served the purpose of the matrix number (q.v.) and vice-versa. Some early double-sided records, notably German G & Ts and Deutsche Grammophons, have a different catalog number on each side, so that the record presumably had to be ordered from the manufacturers by quoting both sides' numbers.

COMMERCIAL RELEASE. A record bearing a normal label, with full details of title, composer, artist, matrix, and/or catalog numbers, and so on, designed for sale in stores. (See also TEST PRESSING.)

CONTROL NUMBER. The number allocated by a company leasing a master for pressing from another company, in addition to or instead of the original matrix number allocated by the parent company, as a means of identification in the files of the leasing company. This was a common practice among the smaller companies that customarily leased masters from such as Paramount, Emerson, Gennett, and Plaza (see chapter 7). From 1901 to 1934, European and Australian HMV also allocated to each master a number by which it could be identified, regardless of whether it had been made by a particular branch or by Victor. Originally this number served as a catalog number, but it was continued on both label and wax in addition to the matrix number, the latter appearing on the wax only. (See also MATRIX NUMBER.)

CYLINDER. The earliest form of sound recording was done on a wax cylinder, slightly tapering, usually about six inches long. These were produced by Edison and his subsidiary companies; Columbia, Lambert, Sterling, Indestructible, and Clarion are among the subsequent makes from the years 1890-1910.

DUBBING. The process of transferring the sound from one disc to another, or from film, tape, or cylinder to one another. Usually adopted in 78 days when an existing original stamper, or positive from which a stamper could be made, was not available or was found to be unsuitable for some technical reason. Dubbing from original to master tape, and from tape to LP master, is the normal procedure nowadays when LPs of reissues from 78s are being compiled. Such is the sophistication of this process that it is extremely difficult, if not impossible, to distinguish between the original and the dubbing. However, in the early days, an onrush of surface noise preceding the first recorded sound of the original would invariably indicate that a record was a dubbing. A further audible clue would be the deadened sound of the dubbing. Expert discographers can distinguish a dubbed pressing from an original by sight, because the style of the grooves, the characteristics of the run-off, sometimes the type used to indent or emboss the matrix number, will differ manifestly. A dedicated collector will seldom accept a dubbing in lieu of an original, and the market value of such is usually only minimal compared with that of a fine copy of an original pressing.

ELECTRIC RECORDING. System of recording introduced on a large scale in 1925 by the major labels—Victor and Columbia, and later, Brunswick—involves the use of a microphone and an amplifier. All sound recording since that date has depended on some form of electric recording (or, as Victor called it, orthophonic recording).

FIELD RECORDING. A recording made under abnormal conditions, such as with a portable recording instrument (nowadays tape, in former times by means of a van equipped with turntables, microphones or horns, cutting devices, and so on). Much valuable recording of folk music, blues, jazz, and other forms has been done "in the field," that is, in the homes of the artists themselves or in makeshift studios in church halls, dance halls, hotel ballrooms, or even bedrooms hired and adapted for the purpose, back rooms of stores, garages, town halls, civic auditoriums, concert halls and, in the case of some Library of Congress recordings of prison songs, in the prisons themselves. During the early days of electric recording —from 1925 to 1930, or thereabouts—much recording was done in America and Europe in churches, cathedrals, and theaters. In the latter case, there were recordings made during performances on the stage in an attempt to create natural realism, and one of the first successes of the electric system was the recording of a chorus of 850 voices and an audience estimated at four thousand, in the Metropolitan Opera House in New York (Columbia, March 31, 1925). Nor was this the first time the "Met" had been the scene of a field recording: the late Lionel Mapleson, a director of the Opera House, secreted a cylinder phonograph in the cat-walk over the stage, equipped it with a recording stylus and as large a horn as was practicable, and captured for posterity as much as he could of the voices of such great stars as Nellie Melba, Pol Plançon, Marcella Sembrich, and Jean de Reszke during their performances there in the seasons of 1901 and 1903. Nellie Melba's farewell to Covent Garden, London, was officially recorded there in 1926, and two years later, a performance of *Boris Godounov* with Fedor Chaliapin was also engraved on wax. An attempt was made on November 11, 1920, to record the ceremony of the burial of the Unknown Warrior in Westminster Abbey, London, by electrical means, but this early field recording was a complete failure. The sound is so badly recorded it did not give more than the merest suggestion of human voices singing.

FINISHED PRESSING. Synonymous with commercial release, q.v.; a copy of record destined for, or having been sold in, a recognized record or other store. (See also TEST PRESSING.)

GRADING. A matter of great importance when buying secondhand records in auctions, from dealers' lists, and so forth. Since the internationally-accepted code of grading was introduced in 1942, by the now-defunct collectors' magazine, *The Record Changer*, most collectors abide by its definitions of the various conditions in which used records of any kind may be found. The following are the grading code letters:

N—the record is absolutely unused, factory fresh. As one eminent collector remarked wryly, "there must be very few 78s in this condition today," although it is still possible very occasionally to track down unsold stock that has been untouched and stored under ideal conditions, so that it still presents the same appearance as when it left the factory decades ago.

E—excellent condition, despite having been played; used with care in every way, so that listening is fully pleasurable and satisfactory. There may be slight marks on the surface, due to damp, rubbing against other records in covers, and so forth, but these make no difference to the reproduction.

V—ostensibly very good condition, but open to very loose definition in practice. Obvious signs of wear include scratches, needle damage of a minor nature, contributing to a somewhat distorted performance (especially on worn loud passages), or a background of needle hiss, clicks, sudden explosions, cracking effects, and sometimes an uneven swishing sound due to part of the track having been exposed to heat. Normally, however, a record in V condition should give reasonably good results.

G—euphemistically known as "good," but in practice rarely what the word normally implies. A G condition record can be expected to have all the defects described in the last paragraph above, on a much greater scale, and a considerable amount of patient adjustment of scratch-filters and other controls on a modern player is needed to produce even reasonable listening.

F—fair, usually implying that there is not much pleasure to be gained from listening to a record in this condition. However, if one is only interested in obtaining a rough idea of what can be expected from a better copy, for future reference should such a copy ever be found, a record in F condition may conceivably satisfy one's curiosity.

P—poor; and as has been said of such a condition, listening is simply not worthwhile, as the wear, tear, damage, and general misuse have rendered the unfortunate record all but unplayable.

It is common practice to make hairline divisions between the upper bracket grades by using plus and minus signs; therefore, a record known to have been played carefully a few times, so that it still looks and sounds as it did the first time it was played, may be described as N —. A record in V — condition can safely be treated with the gravest suspicion and misgivings, but one described as E — may well be considerably better than one graded V or V +.

HILL-AND-DALE RECORDING. The colloquial term for a vertical-cut recording, q.v.

LAMINATION. The process adopted throughout its 78 career by Columbia, and all its subsidiaries (OKeh, Harmony, and others), on a limited scale by English HMV (1927 to 1929), and uniformly by Australian HMV. The grooves are pressed into a thin celluloid plastic coating a tough inner disc made of mica compound, coated with very thin paper. The resultant record is more durable than most made by the "solid stock" process, although the outer coating is liable to crack very easily. Unless the cracking is deep enough to break the inner core, however, this rarely makes any difference to the sound. The principal drawback to lamination is the rumble it tends to impart to the reproduction. However, it is possible to find copies of laminated records in truly misused condition that will nevertheless give a much better account of their music than a "solid stock" pressing in the same or even better condition.

LATERAL-CUT. Most 78s and all LPs and 45s, until the coming of stereo, answer to this description. The sound is recorded on the *walls* of the groove, and the track is cut so that the vibration moves the cutting stylus and the reproducing agent from side to side, instead of up and down as in a vertical ("hill-and-dale") cut. Stereo records are cut with the sound on the walls and the bottom of the track, and the stylus used for playing them impinges on both. The sound waves are relayed to two speakers through an amplifier, one on the left, the other on the right, to create an illusion of balance and expanse. (See also VERTICAL-CUT).

LOCATION RECORDING. See FIELD RECORDING; a location recording is usually one undertaken in a studio in some city where the company does not have a regular studio. As with a field recording, the studio may be a converted room, or it may be a radio station fully equipped for the purpose.

LOCKED GROOVE. Many makes of record since 1923, and most since about 1927, have a spiral groove at the end of the track, and of course all microgrooves and post-1934 78s have this feature also. But quite a number of the older type have the last turn of the playing groove locked into a concentric ring, beyond which a heavy soundbox or pickup should not move. In practice, however, it was found—by some companies such as Columbia, surprisingly, a little belatedly—that the needle or stylus would refuse to remain in the locked groove and would travel across the smooth part around the label, into the label itself, defacing it with a spiral cut in the paper. In very unfortunate cases, the impetus of the motor was sufficient to propel the tone-arm or pickup across the label to the opposite edge of the record, ripping up the track as it did so. The introduction of the automatic brake and the almost universal acceptance of some form of spiral groove at the end of the track eliminated this danger.

MASTER. The original recording, from which copy masters, positives, and negative stampers can be "grown" by electrolytic process. (See also STAMPER.)

MATRIX NUMBER. A vital, essential part of any discography, at least of 78 rpm recordings, the matrix number is allocated to each side by the company making the record, usually at the time of recording, sometimes a day or two in advance. As a rule it is to be found handwritten (etched), embossed, or stamped into the surface of the record, on the smooth un-grooved area around the label, or sometimes under the label and showing through it. (In the latter case, the degree to which the matrix number can be read depends to some extent on the make of record. Pathé records have their matrix numbers indented by hand in tiny figures that can easily be misread. Vocalion did likewise, up to 1924, after the end of which they are no longer visible.)

Usually, the matrix number is a rough guide to the date of recording. If, for example, you wish to determine the recording date of an operatic aria bearing a certain matrix number, and you have details of a popular song or dance record numbered close to it, it is usually quite easy to determine at least approximately the date at which the popular number was being made by all the competing companies. It is, of course, impossible to guess the date of a Victor record that shows no matrix number anywhere at all, but in certain cases where a Victor title was issued in Europe or Australia, the central area on which full details were inscribed at the time of the session is allowed to remain (Victor removed it in the process of pressing), and provides a microcosm of discography in itself.

Nor can companies as colossal as Victor and Columbia be relied on to allocate their matrix numbers in strict chronological order. Most large companies allocated blocks of numbers to their various studios, some of which would exhaust their allocation quicker than others, and thus jump to the next unallocated block, perhaps thousands of numbers further ahead of those of the slower-moving studios.

Experienced discographers and collectors usually become adept at recognizing the typeface used by companies to imprint the matrix numbers on their records and can therefore recognize them in turn if and when they are found on subsidiary labels or overseas issues. Many commit to memory the various blocks of numbers, and a rough estimate of the dates during which they were in use, so that they can be sure of the origin of almost any worthwhile record presented for their inspection.

MULTITRACK RECORDING. The normal record has its sound re-corded on the walls or the bottom of the single spiral groove (stereo records use both), but since the turn of the century, there have been various attempts at producing a "novelty" record by recording on three grooves in close spiral formation, so that it is impossible to predetermine what sound will be produced when the pickup is lowered.

ORIGINAL. The first appearance of a record from the master, not one that has been dubbed, q.v., or reissued, q.v. Such a record can be recognized with practice by the style of print or the design on the label, the type of run-off, the matrix number, or the method used to inscribe it in the wax. An original record does not have to have been issued within the customary few weeks of recording; nor issued in a country other than that of its origin within a short time of its appearance in that country. For example, a record issued in England for the first time six years after it was issued in America is still an original, and should be valued as such, as long as it was pressed from an original stamper.

PIRATE EDITION. An issue of a record of some artistic or historic value by a firm owning no rights to it. By law, a record only passes into public domain fifty-one years after the end of the year in which it was recorded. Thus, if a record was made on January 2, 1935, it will not become public domain until one minute past midnight on January 1, 1986, and anyone other than the parent company or their legal assigns issuing it *in any form* before that date is committing an act of piracy.

PRIVATE RECORDING. There are countless recording studios all over the world that specialize in making records of amateur and sometimes professional artists for their customers' own interest or amusement, as gifts to friends of the performer, or as "demo-discs" to play for influential figures in show business in an attempt to convince them of the excellence of their performance. Major companies have often made private recordings, also. The artist pays a recording fee, for studio and technicians' time, and an agreed number of pressings, perhaps. As a rule, such records are of unintentional humorous value, or of no interest to anyone except the performer and his or her family and friends. The major companies over the years, however, have made records of artists who have gone forward in their professional careers into the world of stardom, and their privately-made, limited-edition records naturally acquire an aura of desirability among collectors and admirers of the artists' later and more famous work. Such records should be included in any professional discography of the artist concerned, or of the kind of performer he or she may be.

PROCESSING DATE. Pathé records pressed in Europe, whether bearing their own or some subsidiary or semiprivate label, invariably show on the run-off, in mirror-writing, a date which many collectors and some discographers have assumed to be the recording date. It is not; it merely indicates the date on which the stamper used for the individual pressing was processed. I have this on the authority of an elderly ex-employee of Pathé in London, whose writing it is. Among the Pathé pressings bearing this date are those on Brunswick, Actuelle, Ideal-Scala, Salabert, Homochord, Sterno, and Labour Leader.

REISSUE. Any record appearing for other than the first time, in any form, is a reissue. As long as a workable master or stamper is used, a reissue can sometimes produce even better results than an original, if the wax used is of superior quality, for example. Many reissues are dubbings, however, q.v., and very inferior to originals. See also ORIGINAL.

REJECT(ED). The recording files of the companies still in existence as a rule divulge the fate of each "take" of a performance, and the usual description of one not accepted, quite logically, is "rejected." (Sometimes the reason for rejection is given; this can make hilarious reading, although doubtless the artists might not agree.) Some discographers use the word "unissued" to denote that a performance was never issued at all, but in the case of 78s, if one of these was never used for merchandise, surely it can be fairly said to have been rejected, at least as a 78, since these have not been produced as commercial artifacts since 1960. Many takes are described as "hold" or "H 30" (meaning "hold for thirty days from the date of the session"), but as no copies of such as these have been discovered in half a century or more, these too can safely be regarded as rejected.

RILL. The groove on a microgroove record linking the end of one track with the beginning of the next.

RUN-OFF. The spiral groove connecting the last concentric groove of the track with an inner groove, which may be concentric with the latter and of course the label, or, in many 78s, eccentric. The eccentric groove was first introduced in 1923 by Victor. HMV began using it at the very end of acoustic recording in 1925, and when EMI was formed in 1931, all labels conformed to a single eccentric ring (as distinct from Victor and HMV's double ring) with a run-off spiral. See also LOCKED GROOVE.

SESSION MAN. A musician employed on an ad hoc basis to provide accompaniment for soloists, or to participate in casual sessions. Often on a semipermanent payroll of one of the major companies, he would be expected to be on call to play any kind of music at sight, sometimes even without written music as such. He would rarely be a *sideman*, a member of a regular orchestra or instrumental group making frequent public appearances in theaters, concert halls, ballrooms, cabarets, and clubs.

SPLICING. The process of joining two pieces of recorded tape together, usually as a result of removing some unwanted section of the original, due to foreign noise, a musical error, or, in the case of dubbing a damaged original, the sound of a persistent click.

STAMPER. The negative (ridged) disc, plated metal to withstand intense heat and pressure, from which playable commercial records are made. Each stamper as a rule bears a code letter or digit, and these of course are visible on the finished pressings. EMI uses a code word, Decca in England a different code word, the letters of which are used in turn as the stampers are brought into use. A pressing bearing two or even three letters in any order is thus one from a stamper obtained from a much-used master; it may give an inferior performance (muzzy sound, swishing surface noise), or it may show no signs of weakening.

SUPPLEMENT. The leaflet issued monthly by most companies, sometimes twice a month in England between the end of the 1920s and the mid-1930s, advertising the new releases of records. Such leaflets are among the most valuable documents a discographer can normally hope to possess, as they provide a firm clue on which to base the recording date. They are often illustrated with most useful photographs of the artists, and sometimes in the sales talk they divulge shreds of information concerning the artist, the actual session that produced the records listed, and even the exact date of that session. Supplements often summarize previously issued records, which of course is also useful in giving a clue to the date beyond which they could not have been recorded.

TAKE NUMBER or DIGIT. Most makes show, after the matrix number or somewhere on the smooth wax surrounding the label, a letter or digit denoting the "take" used for producing the record. Many companies use letters; some, such as Gennett, use no letters for the first take, but take A is the second, take B the third, and so on. Autograph uses the same system, but with digits. Columbia uses digits, at first shown immediately after the matrix number under the label, more recently in the "twelve o'clock" position, with the matrix number at "six o'clock." Victor, not using matrix numbers visibly as a rule, nevertheless usually showed the take digit in the "nine o'clock" position. Edison Bell in England used a peculiarly complex system. The matrix number was followed by a letter denoting the stamper; the take was in the form of a barely visible cipher. Thus: take 1 was a letter X in a circle; take 2, a triangle; take 3, a square; take 4, a horizontal line with a dot either side; and take 5, a circle with a horizontal line through it. (Engineers were instructed that if a satisfactory master could not be obtained in five takes, the whole item was to be abandoned.

Yet Victor frequently made fifteen, twenty, even thirty takes of a single title by one artist. One famous soprano took thirty-eight takes to achieve a satisfactory master of a popular aria.)

TEST PRESSING. A rough "first-off-the-press" record, usually with a plain or at least an undecorated white label, designed to play for the selection committee judging whether or not it was suitable for issue. Such things have a delightful propensity for survival in first-class condition since, having been played a very few times, they often become stacked away in the attic or barn of the committee member who took them home to try them out on his family, perhaps. Sometimes rejects and other fascinating items are found in such places after the demise of their owner.

VERTICAL-CUT. Also known as "hill-and-dale" recording, a vertical-cut record has the soundtrack on the *bottom* of the groove, and the sound-box or, in some rare instances, the pickup rides up and down in it. The louder and deeper the music, the deeper the track. The Buchmann-Meyer effect (q.v.) shown on lateral 78s is very much less in evidence on a vertical-cut, some giving no pattern of this kind at all. Many makes of record started life as vertical-cuts, but all became lateral after it became obvious that this was what pleased the public. Among them, I should mention Brunswick, Vocalion, OKeh, Gennett, Paramount, Pathé, and, of course, Edison. (See chapter 7 for details on these.)

WAX. The inaccurate description of the shellac compound of which most 78s are made. The term is even sometimes applied to the vinylite plastic of which all microgrooves have always been made. It derives from the hard wax block on which the sound was recorded from 1900 to 1950 or thereabouts.

APPENDIX II

Discographical Organizations

IN RECENT years, discography has slowly become recognized as a science worthy of official recognition, and in various parts of the world there are bodies whose aims are the accumulation of objects of value and interest relative to the preservation of recorded sound. These objects are by no means limited to actual records, cylinders, or tapes, but include magazines, ancient and modern, especially those in which the "latest" lists of records are shown as advertising matter, publications frequently or even only occasionally offering works of a discographical nature, as well as the major discographies themselves.

The following is an alphabetical list of the principal organizations devoted to the preservation of such material. It does not pretend to be exhaustive, and it should be understood that there exist many large collections of records and associated memorabilia which are not accessible to the public. (Two that spring to mind are those maintained by EMI Ltd. of Hayes, Middlesex, England, and the British Broadcasting Corporation, London W1A 1AA, England.)

The British Institute of Recorded Sound, 29 Exhibition Road, London SW7 (Director, Dr. Anthony King).

International Association of Sound Archives (President, Dr. Dietrich Schüller, Liebiggasse 5, A-1010 Vienna 1, Austria). An international organization of individuals and institutions concerned with the production of discographical works.

Library of Congress, Washington, D.C., U.S.A. This organization has been making valuable field recordings for many years, several being available for sale. These include work songs, prison songs, blues, hillbilly songs, ethnic group material, and interviews with individuals of outstanding importance, frequently with musical illustrations. The collection of sound recordings has recently been reorganized into a new division, separate from the Music Division which originally directed them.

Nationaldiskoteket Biblioteket, Christiaans Brygge 22, Copenhagen K, Denmark.

National Library of Australia, Music and Sound Recordings Section, Canberra A.C.T., Australia (Director, Peter Burgis). Primarily involved in assembling a complete library of recordings of Australian artists of all kinds, who recorded anywhere in the world.

New York Public Library, New York, U.S.A. This holds a superb collection of vocal records, in addition to reference works and prize rarities of all kinds.

Yale Historical Sound Recordings, Yale University, New Haven, Conn. Largely concerned with rare vocal records, possessing a magnificent collection of these.

Many public libraries throughout the world also hold a representative collection of discographical works such as those discussed in chapter 7.

APPENDIX III

Discographical Magazines

CHAPTER 7 of this book describes in some detail the most generally accepted discographical works that can be fairly described as being of book length, although it must be admitted that several are not much more than booklets or even pamphlets. This appendix covers the magazines known to include as a matter of editorial policy, even on a somewhat irregular basis, discographical chapters on a particular artist, group of artists, or type of recorded music. As with the contents of Appendix II, this should not be regarded as exhaustive. Inevitably the periodicals that publish or have published discographies are themselves specialist by nature, most of them enjoying a relatively small circulation and frequently, alas, rather short-lived. This appendix is not a listing of magazines that review records along with other matters concerning music as a whole, nor those whose raison d'être is to sell records among its subscribers. Such periodicals are of inestimable value to collectors, and the latter often provide in the multitude of lists of records for sale some shreds of information that are discographically interesting or important. An example of this occurred in 1947 in the now-defunct *Record Changer*, when an unissued test pressing of a Paramount record by the great New Orleans jazz cornetist Freddie Keppard was offered to the highest bidder. The strange thing is that nothing more was heard of it, neither its owner nor its winner, if any, ever coming forward to confirm its genuineness or to offer it for issue. Unsuspected alternative takes are often announced in these sales magazines, as are unheard-of additional issues of important collectors' pieces on subsidiary labels to the normal issue. But obviously these worthy publications cannot on these grounds be considered as regular publishers of discographies as defined in the present volume.

The American Record Guide. A monthly magazine that began publication in America in 1935 (from the beginning in May of that year until August 1944 there was some variation in the title). The coverage is mainly classical music.

Antique Phonograph Monthly. An American monthly magazine concerned principally with finding and maintaining old machines, but occasionally discographical features have been published, since the first number in 1973. The editor is Allen Koenigsberg, of 650 Ocean Avenue, Brooklyn, New York 11226, U.S.A.

ARSC Journal. See Association for Recorded Sound Collections Journal.

Asian Music. This American publication is produced twice yearly. As the title suggests, it is concerned with Asian music on record, but discographies are irregular in appearance.

Association for Recorded Sound Collections Journal. Edited by Michael H. Gray, this excellent magazine publishes discographies on an irregular basis, covering mostly classical music. (It features articles on all aspects of recordings, but its appearance is irregular also.) It first appeared in 1967, and is published from P.O. Box 1643, Manassas, Virginia 22110, U.S.A.

Audio and Record Review. This was a British monthly magazine that appeared from 1961 to 1969, concerned mostly with classical music.

Bax Society Bulletin. A British periodical, appearing irregularly from 1968 to 1973, devoted, needless to say, to the music of Sir Arnold Bax.

Coda. Canda's principal jazz magazine frequently publishes chapters of discographical importance from P.O. Box 87, Station J, Toronto, Ontario M4J 4X8, Canada. Appearance is somewhat irregular.

Commodore. This appeared quarterly in Britain between 1971 and 1974. It was named after the Commodore Theatre in Hammersmith, London, and it was principally concerned with light music on 78s. Its discographical contributions were mainly in the form of label discographies. It has been superseded by *Vintage Light Music,* q.v.

Diapason. This French monthly magazine first appeared in 1956 and is mainly concerned with classical music. It has published a number of discographies through the years, but on an irregular basis.

Disc. This was a British quarterly journal that concerned itself in the main with classical music between 1947 and 1953.

Discophile. A mimeographed bi-monthly that began publication in 1948 in England, but after eleven years it became known as *Matrix.* As its title suggests, it contains little other than discographical material, always on some aspect of jazz in all its forms. The editor is George Hulme, of Hayes, Middlesex, England.

Discoteca. An Italian magazine mostly devoted to classical music, but in several of its ten annual issues since 1960 there have been occasional discographies.

Disk. A monthly, mainly classical music magazine published in Holland since 1967, which has featured discographical work from time to time.

Ethnomusicology. A self-explanatory publication, appearing three times a year in the United States, since 1953, containing a regular feature entitled "Current Bibliography and Discography."

Fono Forum. First appeared in 1956; a German, mainly classical magazine that has published some discographies.

Gramophone. Britain's longest-lived monthly magazine devoted to current affairs in the record world, which although largely concerned with matters classical, has always given fair coverage to other forms of recorded music, including discographical material of great value. The first issue was in April 1923. The present publisher and managing editor is Anthony Pollard, and the offices are at 177-179 Kenton Road, Kenton, Middlesex, England.

Gramophone Record Review. A British monthly magazine that lived from 1953 to 1961, covering mostly classical music, occasionally featuring discographies, and superseded by *Record Review*, q.v.

Le Grand Bâton. Despite its French name, this is an American publication, the journal of the Sir Thomas Beecham Society. It has appeared irregularly since 1964, and covers only classical music, with obvious emphasis on that of Sir Thomas Beecham.

The Gunn Report. A British bi-monthly, first appearing in 1968, published by John and Carole Gunn, Hadleigh, Benfleet, Essex, England, and although half of each issue is concerned with lists of records offered for auction, the other half regularly offers discographical features of major importance in the popular music sphere, notably that of prewar years.

Hi-Fi News. A British monthly, commencing publication in 1956, concerned only with classical music and occasionally featuring discographical matter.

Hi-Fi Stereophonie. This German monthly is devoted to classical music, and in the years since its inception in 1962, some discographies have been published.

High Fidelity. An American magazine giving general coverage to current records, on a monthly basis, and which in the years since its first appearance in 1951 has published discographies irregularly.

Hillandale News. A British periodical appearing irregularly since 1960, concerned largely with label discographies, occasionally with music hall artists.

Immortal Performances. Published by Jim Cartwright of P.O. Box 8316, 3007 Fruth Street, Austin, Texas 78712, U.S.A. This is mainly a sales and auction list of classical records (including operatic items), but it has published some first-class discographies of artists coming within that scope.

Jazzfinder—see *Playback.*

Jazz Forum. A short-lived British magazine published by Albert McCarthy, Delphic Press, Fordingbridge, Hampshire, England, in the three or four years following the end of World War II. Some quite useful discographical material could be found amid the tightly set double-column layout of articles with a strangely-orientated political flavor and avant-garde poetry.

Jazzfreund. Germany's principal jazz magazine that has often given space to discographical matters, published from 575 Menden (Sauerland), Schlesienstrasse 11, Germany.

Jazz Journal International. Originally published in May 1948 as simply *Jazz Journal*, this is a British monthly magazine printed on glossy paper, copiously illustrated, quite the longest running jazz magazine in Britain. Discographical works have occasionally appeared.

Jazz Monthly. Similar to the foregoing in style, but with some of the left-wing flavor of *Jazz Forum* lingering (it superseded that paper in 1954), the policy of *Jazz Monthly* allowed for regular discographical contributions, many of which were and are of considerable value.

Jazz Music. One of the very irregularly produced small magazines that proliferated in Britain during the war (in this case, 1942). This was one that continued for a number of years after the end of hostilities, and which published discographical works and articles containing much useful information for the compilation of jazz discographies.

Jazz Tempo. Beginning as a mimeographed booklet of foolscap size, in 1942 in London, England, this evolved into a series of booklets of irregular appearance but invariably containing discographies of jazz and blues (and sometimes popular) musicians, before it ceased publication sometime about 1947.

JEMF (John Edwards Memorial Foundation) *Quarterly.* An American periodical devoted to folk rock, cowboy, Western, gospel, and some blues music. It began publication in 1965, five years after the death, at the age of twenty-eight, of the Australian devotee of country-and-Western music, John Edwards, in a car accident.

Journal of Country Music. An American publication, more or less quarterly, first published in 1969 by William Ivey, Country Music Federation, 4 Music Square East, Nashville, Tennessee 37203, U.S.A. Some suitable discographies have appeared in it.

Journal of Jazz Studies. Appearing twice yearly since 1972, this is an American magazine that frequently features discographies, usually on a "modern" track.

Luister. A Dutch classical monthly, beginning in 1952. Irregular appearances of discographies have been featured in it.

Matrix. The mimeographed magazine that took over *The Discophile* in January 1959, and which has since published, at bi-monthly intervals, an impressive array of discographies of all kinds of jazz subjects, often of a "Modern" kind. (See also *The Discophile.*)

Memory Mail. A short-lived British monthly publication that began in 1972 and was mainly interested in popular music, giving occasional discographical articles.

Music Hall Records. A bi-monthly British magazine with a self-explanatory title, published by Anthony Barker, 50 Reperton Road, London S.W.6, England. It has featured regular discographical articles each issue since the first in 1978.

Musica. An Italian quarterly, beginning in 1977 and covering opera and classical music, with occasional discographical features.

Musica e Dischi. A similar Italian magazine to the above, but of much longer establishment. It first appeared in 1945 and in its monthly issues since, there have been irregular discographical contributions.

New Amberola Graphic. American quarterly, first published on a regular basis in 1972 by Martin F. Bryan, 37 Caledonia Street, St. Johnsburg, Vermont 05819, U.S.A. A valuable periodical that habitually lists discographical material never before published anywhere, and of all kinds.

Opera. This British monthly first appeared in 1950, and has since published irregular discographies.

Phono. A bi-monthly German classical-music magazine that flourished from 1950 to 1966, and sometimes featured discographies.

Phoprisma. Another German classical-music magazine that issued bi-monthly coverage of classical music from 1962 to 1969, and sometimes included discographies in its makeup.

Playback. This was the name by which *Jazzfinder* became known after the first year or so of publication (from January 1948). The final issue was in March 1950, but in that short time, this well-produced magazine offered several interesting discographical features. It was published in New York.

The Record Changer. From 1942 to 1957, this American jazz magazine flourished as a discographical medium as well as a purveyor of very interesting, copiously illustrated, and professionally produced articles on all kinds of jazz, mainly the classic kind, and as an auction room for collectors to bid on the thousands of records offered each issue.

The Record Collector. A pocket-sized, glossy-paged printed magazine published by James F.E. Dennis, 17 St. Nicholas Street, Ipswich, Suffolk, England, since 1950. Publication is somewhat irregular, but discographies of opera singers of all periods of recorded history are a regular feature.

Record Research. Published by Len Kunstadt and Bob Colton from 65 Grand Avenue, Brooklyn, New York 11205, since 1955, this excellent magazine makes a point of all kinds of discographical features appearing regularly in its pages, jazz, ancient and modern, side by side with country-and-Western, nostalgic-popular artists, blues, and label listings. There are many illustrations and much discographically slanted detail given in the other articles. It appears bi-monthly.

Record Review. This British classical-music magazine superseded *Gramophone Record Review* (q.v.) in 1957, but ceased publication in 1970. It was a monthly, and sometimes presented discographical material.

Recorded Sound. The quarterly "house" magazine of the British Institute of Recorded Sound, 29 Exhibition Road, London SW7, England. Since 1961 it has featured a number of very varied discographical contributions.

Rhythm Rag. A sales magazine that includes discographical material, published quarterly by Dave and Pat Cunningham from 190 Camrose Avenue, Edgware, Middlesex, England, since spring 1976. Mainly a medium for features on various aspects of recording artists of the past, of all kinds, with no special emphasis on jazz, rhythm, or ragtime music.

Shellac Stack. An auction sales list published quarterly by Paul C. Burgess, Box 252, Friendship, Maine 04547, U.S.A., but one which includes excellent jazz discographical features, with illustrations of good quality.

Stereo Review. An American publication appearing monthly since 1967, covering classical music and sometimes featuring discographies.

Storyville. Britain's principal jazz magazine, whose policy allows no reference to postwar "developments" (bop, modern jazz, cool jazz, and so forth), but which produces beautiful bi-monthly issues, finely illustrated, and usually including some in-depth discographical features. It is published by Storyville Publications & Co. Ltd., 66 Fairview Drive, Chigwell, Essex IG7 6HS, England.

Talking Machine Review. A British bi-monthly, excellently produced and copiously illustrated, dealing with early recording artists, their work, and details of the records they made, along with early machines. There are often label listings also. Published by Ernest Bayly, 19 Glendale Road, Bournemouth, Dorset BH6 4JA.

Vintage Light Music. The successor to *Commodore,* this British magazine was first published in 1975, covering light music on 78s on a rather irregular basis. Discographies are occasionally included.

INDEX

About the Author

BRIAN RUST is a professional discographer and recording historian. One of the pioneers of discography, his many previous works include *Recorded Jazz: A Critical Guide, The Complete Entertainment Discography*, the *American Record Labels Book, Jazz Records, 1897-1942, The American Dance Band Discography, 1917-1942*, and *Discography of Historical Records on Cylinders and 78s*. (Greenwood Press, 1979).